# Speaking in Tongues

## Selected Poems

# Speaking in Tongues

## Selected Poems

# H.C. ten Berge

*Translated by* Pleuke Boyce

*With an Afterword by* Breyten Breytenbach

Ekstasis Editions

Published in 2021 by:
Ekstasis Editions Canada Ltd.
Box 8474, Main Postal Outlet
Victoria, B.C. V8W 3S1

Ekstasis Editions
Box 571
Banff, Alberta T1L 1E3

LIBRARY AND ARCHIVES CANADA CATALOGUING IN PUBLICATION

Title: Speaking in tongues : selected poems / H.C. ten Berge ; translated by Pleuke Boyce with an afterword by Breyten Breytenbach.
Other titles: Poems. Selections (2021)
Names: Berge, H. C. ten, 1938- author. | Boyce, Pleuke, 1942- translator. | Breytenbach, Breyten, writer of afterword.
Description: Poems in English; translated from the Dutch.
Identifiers: Canadiana (print) 20210125616 | Canadiana (ebook) 20210125691 | ISBN 9781771714167
(softcover) | ISBN 9781771714174 (ebook)
Classification: LCC PT5881.12.E65 A2 2021 | DDC 839.313/64—dc23

Canada Council    Conseil des Arts
for the Arts      du Canada

Ekstasis Editions acknowledges financial support for the publication of *Speaking in Tongues* from the Nederlands Letterenfonds // Dutch Foundation for Literature, from Government of Canada through the Canada Book Fund and the Canada Council for the Arts, and from the Province of British Columbia through the Book Publishing Tax Credit.

Printed and bound in Canada.

*I taste a thousand times the poem that is not*
*on the lips, I put my face a thousand times*
*in my hands and think of Bashō*
   *whose name a rustling of leaves,*
*who only wanted the simplest,*
*let the unreachable nearby*
   *keep its form*
*so that light and reed, frog and lotus*
*were for an instant understood in their forlornness*
*and I can take his poem on the lips a thousand times,*
*can after three hundred years in the east*
*or the west of the country read the poem from his lips,*
*the lips of Bashō*
*who travelled and knew:*
   *this I have chosen*
*with the exclusion of everything else.*

From: *Materia Prima, Poems 1963-1993*

# Contents

From *Materia Prima, Poems 1963-1993*

The White Shaman, An Initiation  / 11
The White Shaman, The Other Sleep  / 18
Texan Elegy I, *Empty stage under grey skies*  / 25
Texan Elegy II, A Tomb for Ezra Pound  / 28
Texan Elegy V, *Kill your darlings, poet!*  / 36
Texan Elegy IX, *Thrown out of his landscape*  / 40
Texan Elegy XIII *Begin, write – behold*  / 42
Apple Beach  / 43
Fernando Pessoa reads the dispersed limbs of Juan de la Cruz  / 45
Album by Kao Ch'i-P'ei  / 46
Nemrud Dagh  / 48
We dream away in blue and grey (A Triptych for Max Beckmann)  / 50
The Surrounding and Nearby  / 54

From *Cantus Firmus,* Poems 1993-2013; *Splendor* (2016)
& *Speaking in Tongues* (2020)

Cantus Firmus (a selection)  / 63
A Gust of Wind in August  / 74
September  / 76
Winter Sentence  / 77
On Piazzolla Street  / 78
Time Is  / 84
*Three metamorphoses*
    En Toute Candeur  / 85
    The Enchanted Ship  / 87
    Kingfisher at Sea  / 89
The Great Disdain, A Fable  / 90

Nansen on The Ice Sea   / 98
Whip-Shaped Sermon   / 102
Introverted Sermon   / 104
Sermon for Deaf Ears   / 106
What I saw and underwent   / 109
*Five Dances of Death:*
    In The Year of The Plague (1964)   / 111
    Lübeck (1965)   / 113
    Dança Mortal (1977)   / 115
    Dancemaster Death (2013)   / 117
    The Hour Glass (2016)   / 119
I Fly Through The Thirteenth Century   / 121
Amstel Station 9.1.76 / 9:15   / 129
Arnout of Ribérac Sees His Forbidden Love from Afar   / 131
Splendor (a selection)   / 132
*Field Notes from Underground:*
    Speaking In Tongues (a fragment)   / 139
    Of the Fire God and the Mortal (I)   / 141
    Of the Fire God and the Mortal (II)   / 142
    Lost in Mictlan   / 145
    The Four Hundred Hares   / 148
Tramontane   / 154

*Breyten Breytenbach:*
Nine Good Reasons Why I Cannot Write An Introduction   / 157

Translator's acknowledgments   / 163
About the Author   / 165
About the Translator   / 166
About Breyten Breytenbach   / 167

Poems from
*Materia Prima*

# An Initiation
*The White Shaman (I)*

1

Flying in over the Sont,
over dark bowls of Finnish lakes.

Boarding the kayak
of the departed.

Drifting on the waters
between taiga and tundra.

Purging eye and ear
in emptiness and expanse.

Feeding on berries, on cap
and scent of the divine mushroom.

Dreaming the dream
of the eternal present.

As an arctic bear
retiring into snowblind drunkeness again.

2

Melting seven snow flakes on the tongue
in waning afternoon light.

Crawling into his tent
when the sleepy sun sinks behind the woodlands.

Lying on a bed of leaves
fanning the smouldering fire of birch bark.

Spying on the white-blue Pole Star
through the smoke hole.

Watching in pure joy the heavenly nail
and shining navel of the universe.

Leaving the tent on all fours
for the distant swoosh of a wingbeat.

To stand eye to eye with the white wolves
of a brief dawn.

3 *Initiation*

The Great Mother flies
between Ural and Altai.

To grow rigid between her feathers and sleep
the death sleep of the shaman.

Her throat is a drum,
her throat becomes his vulnerable voice.

From the drum: raw cackling of reindeer-koryaks,
the hoofbeat, the rolling call of Yakuts on horseback.

Snow is on his lips,
foam covers the ground.

From her breast the birch tree grows
and the sleeper shelters in its upper branches.

A beak pecks at his groin,
an eagle feather trembles in the wind.

4

To wound oneself to be reborn
unharmed and clear.

Roughly toppled out of the egg
by the waving mother who flies away.

The first snow has fallen; a fresh game trail
leads from the forest's edge to here.

Oh children of Nanook
he returns with his song.

Nails of ice stand in the cortex of knowing.
The lips are cold but the tongue is purified.

Who brings light? Who healing?
He has been carried around the world seven times.

His hair, like a hat,
is pierced with a flight feather.

## 5  *First song of the shaman*

'Slender she is, small like a baby bear,
she shakes her black braids like wings,

her calico smock
is hanging from a branch.

In the breathing house of skin and wood
my cosmic axle churns deep inside her womb.

Nipples taut, skin in bloom,
snow rubbed into a blush on her thighs.

Oh, look like a mouse
through the eye of the tent!

How Nanook's daughter as snow goddess still rocks,
softly humming under my fur.

Tempting scent of eternal present, now that
seven days have proven to be seven years already.'

6

Mirage of cities, fleeting props
in the empty chaos of the steppe.

Living with few signs
embodying his total lostness:

Pole Star, Pleiades, the hunt
of the hounds, swift as arrows.

Weakened by resin, hash and millions
of mosquitoes, he slides down the tree.

He imagines
disappearing into the other tree,

concludes
that both have vanished.

Next to the shaman the scrawny hunter; behind them
the woman who, on her haunches in the grass, drops a thirsty cub.

7

Oh brothers and sisters, the blossoming of the imagination
is taking a long time.

It's not easy to speak
the snow language of the Samoyeds

nor is it easy to attach an image
of restrained emotion

to secret or domestic violence,
the rasping bombast of a civilization.

The white shaman becomes a crippled leper
who traverses colonies with his shrill rattle.

The game trail disturbed,
the fruit bud poisoned.

Who has dismantled
which innate power –

# The Other Sleep
*The White Shaman (II)*

1

Grey light, late swans in a straight flight
          along the thin outlines of retreating mountains.

Having come on the celestial horse from Fergana
          and now on the edge of frozen marshes.

To the south the road that branches off on the autumnal tableland:
          image of vapour around mounted nomads,

the flash of a train, red and dusty, breaking from the mountain flanks –
          and low, in the western basin, the yellow yolk of the sun.

Brought by guides, ill-practiced but well
          equipped, I sit on moss among skinny birches.

I poke in the ash of an ancient fireplace;
          wet nostrils, eyebrows bristly with frost.

Too late an early snow hare gets wind
          of the preying fox.

2

Here regarded as a fool
        there excluded as a grimface

I claim to know of nothing else
        than what is or was created by my hand;

having remained ignorant through thinking,
        in everything a novice who unlearns

and then attempts again
        to start a fire of damp wood.

Creaking, moaning, nevertheless
        digging into dreams for ancestral forms:

Roasted the hare after all! but then with spit
        as angle bar carried tentward

by curious hunters (who had heard a rumour
        that the tsar was murdered long ago).

3

That's going to be something when the revolution
          of the estranged breaks out in the city!

Although recovered, the body falters
          in immense emptiness

and obscene silence fells the spirit
          like a birch;

oh cool womb-like earth,
          even the pliable spear of the slow

and distant sun chafes your skin here like a pebble
          skipping over water.

The cold of ages keeps the earth's crust
          in summer and winter sedated –

only death gets through to her;
          the rustling of rats swells in the shrubs.

4

Troubled, in his tent on the mount
        lies the stubborn sucker from the west

who only sleeps to find
        the essence of sleep,

who, thinking of sunken lives
        slowly sinks down into the dark tidal forest below.

The sopping wet plains solidify,
        the growing frost opens up the marshes;

fur hunters shoot him awake: dragged along
        into which present? did they hit upon an ancient

catch in the bog? (Dead mammoths still bear living
        germs of anthrax under their skin;

bat-grey and musty like sheep the meat
        will strike the eager eaters with eternal sleep.)

5

Remember images of people
        tough and supple like a spine:

the Windeby Girl – she with the blindfold
        strangled in the bog and tanned

like a cow's hide between oak bark;
        the red Venus of Yde, corpse full of grease;

the Grauballe Man – caught
        in fear, with damaged throat,

stripped of life
        as a text of its meaning,

but still pinned down with forked sticks
        at the very bottom of the bog

and then covered with willow branches,
        tough and supple like a spine.

6 < IN THE MOSSY BASIN AT THE TREE LINE >

A grave; the slow digging starts,
           layer after layer is steadily cut away:

a soapstone bowl and traces of fire,
           we hit upon signs –

halted language
           scratched into an oracle tooth.

Then, from fault lines in petrified mud
           the shrouded double image of black eyes breaks through

– as from dead lovers, surprised in the act
           of coition and not found again by friends;

brought down by time and chance
           but now a prey to frozen ecstasy –

still expecting birth
           and already into death.

7

Is the raven coming yet?
              is the bear not yet loose?

Here, under the wide-brimmed hat
              of cattle drivers and ministers,

firm in the saddle – the horse fly
              crushed to death on the forehead,

along the road that branches off,
              between retreating pine forest and approaching tableland –

where the wood thins like poet's hair,
              on the border of hoofbeat and heaven's lightning

we say goodbye
              while the sparks are extinguished

and slumber is roused to feed consciousness
              with signs of emptiness and life.

# Texan Elegies I

Empty stage under grey skies,
Time of defence and embraces,
Choked moaning on the inside.

All words have been used.

Begin, write,
          for example
That we are living, they said,
That we are living under a system
And that it's always on the brink
So that we have to guard
What would protect us.

And that's how it began

If need be without speaking
Skill or joy of speech, plagued
For so long by mouth ache
That silence reached the lips
And intestines flushed out grammar for good.

And that is how it will be written,

If need be
Without basis or outlook,
Stripped of body wear
That was left behind like a conscript's shoe
In a startled mine field.

From now on violence is a privilege
Of the state, they said,
Resistance is futile, better get
That through your head, so figure out
What you think you should think
And aren't doing.

Every word
Chewed over and spat on, under pressure
Of the circumstances, wanting
Only the best for you, so don't find
Fault with everything and you'll
Slime your way through it.

Take yourself out of it
or you'll be taken out (they said).

All words have been used –
Break them
And use the dust from ancient metaphors,
Stone Age images
That withstood decay and lip service,
Sentences that kept their suppleness,
Words from the street
That slept exhausted in the sewers.

Leave no blank page
Unspoken to
Like that drunken wall flower
Who brushed herself off under the streamers
Got up muttering, winced,
Crumpled and forgot herself.

Where was that and who
Leaned against the wall as someone
Modelling who then walked away
And came back and walked away again
Like one of those lost figures,
Not knowing why his body was there
At that hour?

Was it
At one of those informal garden parties
With whisky and bitter women
And beer from a keg;
        did you not stand there
Slightly hunched over between clothes pegs and Chinese lanterns
In that indefinable city?

# Texan Elegies II
*A Tomb for Ezra Pound*


Later, and elsewhere, broken
Connections, lost myself too
   'Because my confidence has taken a hit' (she said).
Following Snake River, *famous potatoes*, as far as Twin Falls
Everything green, everything
Windy and waving,
   filled with horses and spuds,
No tree that doesn't bend before the wind,
    for the wind in Shoshone,
Who needs to piss flops down
With a full bladder between bushes, covered in dust,
Who looks for a bar will not find one
Without god's help and some hundred horse powers.

Dizzy in the morning, dead
Beat behind hash-browns
In Hailey, Idaho

Chilly windy weather
The house of Homer P.

'Corrupt strangers'
1944
Pound to Mussolini, later daily
To Mezzasoma in Salò:
Lippmann and the 'Jewspapers', 'the plutocratic
    putrid jewified yankee press'.
Roosevelt, 'the chief war pimp', was filth –
Backed by '60 kikes', 'Stinky Rooosenstein'
    had provoked the war.

Old Ez,
Scriptor cantilenae,
Helluva poet, lost
And dazed in Rapallo;
No road led back
To Idaho,
        asking himself
Why the poets of the new world
Were rarely respected by the people;
Demanding attention like a child
That beats newborn kin to death in the cradle,
Liked speaking
        *de litteris et de armis, praestantibus ingeniis,*
About books and weapons and men of exceptional talents,
'The usual subjects of conversation between intelligent men,'
And yet locked up
For fifteen years with big-time crooks, disturbed at that;
Longer than the last loves of the dead Duce
        des großdeutschen Reiches
Ez wandered, threatened by derangement
In the maze without a thread,
Dante nor Odysseus,
Fed and watched by Yankees.

Rumours, rustlings, word fluff
Blowing around his ears, bits of images
Like tangles in his hair,
A slime mold culture in blind alcoves … 'Ez for Pres!'
'If This Be Treason …'
Voices that grew silent
When his mouth decided
To give up speaking.

*I am not a demigod*

Wrecked ships without Circe
Or Calypso on the coast,
Golden belts and breast bands dull,
Faded shadows on a damp back wall,

*I cannot make it flow thru*

Saw no light swathed in the hills
And no mountain lake in the pale dawn.
Caged delusions, seas without lustre,
No stone, no shard gleamed in a hand.

*I cannot make it cohere*

No splendour of towers, no radiance on water;
Tried the earthly paradise; Perigord or
Provincia Deserta where the singing was good
But word dreams were burned.

*O Artemis, foam and silk are thy fingers*

Sparks, sometimes a flame
    that went out quickly.
Years of deception, then reconciliation –
    Pound and Ginsberg
    in Venice, autumn '67:
Confucius versus Buddha
    (the tired master with excema on raw knuckles
    and a fragile constitution).
'My worst mistake …that stupid, suburban prejudice'
'Lovely to hear you say that'
'I was stupid, also ignorant, I knew nothing'
    And Ginsberg with rabbinical beard
    asked that day for Ezra's blessing.

His gaze stayed sharp, his voice faded.
Death, it seemed, was tying up at the lagoon.

Five autumns later, silently passed away,
Black gondola across the water,
Flowers bent before the wind, that fall day
At the cemetery of San Michele.

Is there at this time a subject
Worthier than the fear
That the races should rise against each other?

The
Beautiful
Contradictions

With Tarn in the Tate, a winter
Ago, stabbing pain in his back
While Turner sent his mists of light
Right through us:
     'We must never close our eyes
To the faults of the master
But, by god, he *is* the master!'

Nose blown, staring
At the outside, through a window,
London grey. Asphalt
Wet.
Black edge around the window sill.
Two dogs at a Belisha beacon,
A cyclist with a trouser clip,
Building-wide slogan
Lit up across the road

HAPPINESS IS A CIGAR CALLED HAMLET

31

Silently on a chair, drowsing,
Nodding, the attendant, deep split
In her skirt, soft, silky glow of
Stockings, blouse, brown hair,
    in the dim light,
My head half turned away,
Reflections of her thighs in a cube
(Maker unknown),
A slow swivel, and again
The view of a reality
That I reluctantly turn my back to.

That Spring, through the hills along Lake Austin, Texas,
Dark, vernal rustling,
Full of deer and hares, dead armadillos
At the roadside. Emir in the back seat
Throwing around sad jokes
('Where I come from, my friend, civilization
advances irreparably'),
Beside me Haroldo, family man, poet
Who sends his words unstoppably ahead
Into the night, past the enchanted rock
And the hills, hungering for verticals,
And further, euphorically
Averse to the uninhabited,
Towards Llano Estacado,
Paving the roads *riso clandestino* with flowers and hearts.

O azul é puro?
O azul é pus

Blue is pure?
Blue is puss

(O fear
for empty stomachs
and provinces)

ANA   FLOR *Du tropfes Tier* read aloud
on 24<sup>th</sup> Street
'Oh thou beloved of my twenty-seven senses…
Blue is the colour of your yellow hair
Red is the cooing of your green bird'

*Klangfarbenmelodie*
'Who have gone before us?
Van Doesburg, Schönberg, Mondrian!'

His goat's laugh cuts through the darkness,
He confesses his abhorrence of emptiness,
Conducts while speaking:
In seas and deserts his letter complexes spring up,
Landscapes are adorned with sentences,
Cities, constructions are marking space,
The symmetry of signs
Rythmically strewn out into the unknown.
Tested by eye and ear
The poem is only settled in his mouth.

Haroldo and Noigandres:
'Noigandres, eh *noi*gandres,
Now what the DEFFIL can that mean?'

Travelled to Italy to shake the hand of old Ez
The way he once visited Freiburg im Breisgau
To interrogate the spry old Lévy about Provençal songs.

From Sâo Paulo to the Brunnenburg, Merano,
Only took an eternity.

Noigandres, by god
What can that mean.

Idling at a crossroads without signs,
In the distance Bobwhite whistles his name too late.
A ball of spit flies out the window.

'Schwitters and the style have gone before'

A blue flower grows
Out of concrete,
Thick fingers
Plucking at his beard,
The car is gaining speed, wheels
Humming at the bend,
Emir fights a hangover with silence.
'And yet,' the poet snarls
While snakes, raccoons and hares collapse under the tires
'Pound was my university!'

First a gasping little laugh
Then, his bleating, full-throated roar.

Engine off and radio on.
Fiddling and warbling from pinched throats.
Thin voice in the cab when the descent has started –
'Mother of God, where is this going, amigo?'

Visibility fades
The windshield soon cakes over
With mosquito corpses.

It is as I say, this is
The road to Whisky River.

Eagerly, lips pressed together
We drive up to the water.

**Notes**:

Homer P: father of Ezra Pound

Emir Rodriguez Monegal (1921-1985): influential critic and editor; wrote a literary biography of Jorge Luis Borges.

Haroldo de Campos (1929-2003): Brazilian poet and translator of Pound's *Cantos*. One of the founders of the Noigandres group (which stood for the concretist movement in Brazil) and the experimental journal of the same name.

Ana Flor: Kurt Schwitter's love poem 'Anna Blume'.

Van Doesburg and Mondria(a)n: Dutch artists and founders of the international modernist movement called The Style.

Quotations 1944: taken from Pound's letters to the Italian government.

# Texan Elegies V

Kill your darlings, poet!
Bees crawl between ribs of a rotted carcass;
Was he perhaps a boy with too much yearning
That one day he lost all his honey –

Aristaeus, Tramontane
           (The one begotten
In Libya's golden room,
The other in a cold and narrow bed;
Then truly made a mess of things,
got themselves in trouble,
Wandered around and managed
nothing anymore.)

Alone through the twilight, the stony plain,
Away from the sensitive heart,
Back to the hills and illuminated gardens,
Where bats and angels
Tumble in drums of air,
Beside the road bloody raccoons,
Budweiser, blue bonnets, dozing
Vultures and dead deer,
Teeming of flies,
Their whining buzz stifled.

Went on foot and alone through the twilight.

The eyes empty and filled again
With nothing
But dust, reflections, after-
Images of other eyes in his,
Eyes empty and filled again
With nothing
But tears, daggers, double
Images of his eyes in hers,

Loose eye lashes,
Fingers, wet with slime, between the teeth
And a voice singing from a stereo tower
On a deck above the water
    'I want to stay with you until my death'
    (Sehnsucht).                                    (Longing)

It should be louder (softer),

*Le pouvoir*
        *du chant, Madame*
*La faiblesse*

Humming at the fence
To drown out her sobbing
Between two telephones.

No one ever sang someone back from death.

Stale smell of gas, pink
Oleanders; music in the garden
Sounded like music
Out of passing cars;
Girls in too tight blouses
Arrived, drove
Off, carried
The universe between their legs,
Chewing all the while,
Didn't say a word
That wasn't fit for a balloon.

These aren't songs for ladies,
This is no hog feed for consumption.

Traces of vomit, corners of mouth
Turned down, sour cocktails
In glasses.

His Penelope infuriated
And Calypso far away
He stood for hours with sprained ears
And a plastic laugh
Between clothes pins and Chinese lanterns, slightly
Bent and reined in, hatless
With empty hands     also
Barked at and snarled at
In the mother tongue of fatherless women,
Yet refreshed, invigorated, not
At all deterred,
With a nose for honey
That stubbornly follows the trail
Of her disappearances,
Apparently from ear to ear
Relaxed, even swaying elastically
As if after a meal
With Propertius, Nietzsche, Frau
Von Salomé
        (Oh sensuality
        und Schicksal, Oh                          and fate, oh
        triebhaftes Wesen)                         passionate being
In that indefinable city
Of hedges, clean-shaven
Armpits, checked suits, buttocks
Bulging from too short pants,
Lone Star caps, plaster
Cupids and home computers,
Bottles in paper bags and dented
Cars     in the back yard     azure
Swimming pools and throats of vinegar

That would now, if they may,
Like to point out the inadmissibility
Of certain ideas and commie poets,
Parasites on top of that, sticking like rubber stingers
(Compassion, compassion and murmuring)
In the pale flesh of free democrats,
And how someone in the silence that ensued,
For the last cocktail,
Called for happiness, laughter,
A touching and breaking of glasses,
At which a drunken broad
Took off all her clothes, lifted
With bronze arms, torso and all
Her sorrow ecstatically to the stars –
Then, hit by light shards
Crumpled under a table
 so that Tramontane, with wine
And darts and a thin mouth, between
White telephones bit his lips on the terrace,
While the pain of losing stood
Like a pale reflection in his eyes.


*Aristaeus*:  Greek mythical figure, the first ever beekeeper who lost his bees (and honey)
after casting an eye on Orpheus wife, Eurydice, who was his sister in law.
*Sextus Propertius* (born 48 B.C., died after 16 B.C.): wrote four books of poems, was a
founder of the Roman love elegy.
*Frau von Salomé*: known as Lou Andreas-Salomé (1861-1937), author, psychoanalyst, lover
and idol of many men, admired and loved by Nietzsche and the poet Rainer Maria Rilke
(with whom she visited Russia twice). Published a book on eroticism and physical love. Was
also a friend and confidante of Sigmund Freud.

# Texan Elegies IX

Thrown out of his landscape
    early, he lived slowly
        but in hindsight always too fast.

The mythic place
    was the bridge
        in the land, the light

In the ditch, where pikes
    flashed in those days –, the road one evening
        strewn with toads.

A delayed thunderstorm
    hung over the woods, the clock of the Ursulines
        carried over the meadows

To the violet of a faint horizon;
    the heat did not abate, he lay
        among ground-ivy and clover

And chewed on sorrel
    without looking, but so
        that he still saw everything:

The first ripple
    through unshorn fields,
        empty bunkers

Where thin cries were uttered, high firs
    bent by the wind
        over a half-hidden house.

This was the spot, there
    was the place where he read
        what he later experienced:

A hand on a knee,
    a burr in the hair
        and her bike in the grass.

# Texan Elegies XIII

Begin, write – behold
What you bring about and didn't plan
What was done, you sometimes did
      from love, sometimes from needing to survive

Through the word's blind germinating power.
But does it also bear a name and did it get
That shape of what one calls Whale, Wolverine, Wise
      Woman with a Bloated Body?

Does she always have two faces? One
that speaks, one that remains a blank?
Is it her hidden mouth that lures the seeker,
      quite possessed, to the unknown?

Were you pulled along by her or driven on?
Did she then swallow you and close you in?
How many seas, which shores? How long
      did you drift around in her intestines?

What is it that has touched you in her being
And what has she withheld from you –
She, who had incorporated you
      and cast you out like Jonah on an empty coast?

# Apple Beach / Praia das Maçãs

A high coast in a haze of sleep.

Languid drifters
slide through the sun and the sea-green
dream of lost Americas;

a reef sprays light behind the surf.

Wine on the western slopes,
paths bordered by agaves
and barren fields burned in the valley.

The sharp reed crouches at the springs.

On surrounding hills
the sun smoulders
in dismantled monasteries and forts.

The game was up here
before it even started.

Above the fields
a white moon ripens early,
the salty wind attacks the skin again –
> *goddess on the cactus*
> *goddess in the sand*
> *the stalk of the maize*
> *is growing in your hand!*

At the windows
women and crows rise up,
rise up
and rearrange.

A voice carves
a song in the twilight –

      *goddess on the cactus*
      *goddess in the sand,*
      *my tongue*
             *steals the salt from your lips,*
      *my mouth*
             *drinks the dew from your hand;*

      *child, you know what I want,*
      *I ask for no caresses,*
      *when the wind goes through the maize*
      *it ruffles your tresses!*

The heart is slow and tempestuous.

A spring tide of seed breaks
in the core
of wet caves.

The high coast in a haze of sleep

but the sea
        there
            below
the sea
     there
       below
          foams drunkenly off apple beach.

From: *Va-banque / All or Nothing*

# Fernando Pessoa Reads the Dispersed Limbs
# of Juan de la Cruz


So what should I think of in the middle of December, in the rain?

'...read nearly two pages
Of a mystic poet's book,
And laughed like someone who has wept a lot.'

That Spanish smell of cruelty, the sweet musk
odour in a broom closet that was passing for a cell.

There he was lying, *alumbrado*, all given over to the lust of dying,
With the scent of holiness and eaten by his wounds,
Chased from the mother womb by his lesser masters.

'I'd rather be among stones than among people' –
I wish I'd written that, hidden behind my names.

Robbed of all that he had left: fingers, open
Sores, the bloody rags stuck to an emaciated body,
The soul in heavy rain still barely risen from the unlit night
An admirer, in his eagerness, had bitten off a toe, perhaps
The whole half of a foot.

This is the answer of a Lusitanian:
He wrote too little and too much,
He expounded about a handful of verses and symbols
That would explain the climb to lofty peaks of love.

If only he had turned to stone and had remained a stone.
Stone's mystery would then have been described from the inside.


From: *Overgangsriten / Rites of Passage*

45

## Album by Kao Ch'i-p'ei

The civil servant whose fingers in a dream
contracted into brushes.

The rigid ritual:
the ink first rubbed, then a day's wait.

'My hand starts, there's still nothing there'

The primer brushed and washed –
A mountain path, ducks, trees
applied with nails and fingertips.

Junks under sail, wooded banks,
a tiger, plump, seen from behind.

Go back, oh traveller
the duck flees from the reeds!

The pinkie pats panic
in a wingbeat, a thumb smudge
has the bamboo bow before the wind.

Small boats, vague human outlines
floating on a vast expanse of water.

Uphill a donkey rider, a bent
servant following on foot;
his sighing rises from the paper –

How heavy is the load? How long yet
will he have to lug the folded parasol?

A luminous haze surrounds the distant conifers –
twigs, needles are in greyish blue
carefully nailed against the light.

The climb to the top a steep oppression.

True intuition, flair: everything dead-on
but always given form by touch.

The viewer watches it:
mule, master, servant who motionless
for centuries continue up the hill,

Red seals on the edge of the paper,
an inscription written somewhere
by an unknown hand:

'His fingers moved in total freedom'

Kao Ch'i-p'ei has painted it.
When I am finished, he said,
my nails are gone.

* Kao Ch'i-p'ei (Gao Qipei), an innovative Chinese landscape painter. Lived from 1660–1734.

From: *Overgangsriten / Rites of Passage*

# Nemrud Dagh

Resentfully like ageing bulls the mountains stand
Up to the westerly Euphrates.
Drought carves the roads and marks them with inscriptions,
Right from the base I hitch a ride and think: Mâshallâh,
What a girl! After an hour the car gets stuck
In Commagene where Antiochus the Anatolian
Built a mountain terrace with stone gods.

No cart track and no camel, we are
fucked. Her throat a rasp that's
Spouting wrath; I swallow caustic
Words and whistle a shrill tune
Under the hood. The sun burns
endlessly, unmovable it seems, an almost
Scorching fire above the ridges in the west.

Rubble glows like a stone furnace.

She points at the terrace where eagles
fell to earth and a god, knocked off
his pedestal, now peers into a crack.

Broken eyes
Look out over the dust of ages
And the creatures we pretend to be.

Fault line. We are losing ground under our feet.

A slope suddenly tips over,
Rocks, torsos, weathered faces cascade down.
The earth yawns and gobbles up her rulers.

A blade of light hacks in on us.
The car lies crushed to pieces like a house.
We have escaped, are shocked.

Escaped from walls of dust.

A new god and his goddess:
We stand there, petrified, in shaky balance –
Eternally together and forever alone.

From: *Overgangsriten / Rites of Passage*

# We Deam Away in Blue and Grey
*A triptych for M.B.*


I


Max Beckmann, I admire you!
And Quappi too!
Your women take my breath away
Those shapely thighs, good grief, spell doom for any man.

I throw myself at the paint and force
My way through seven keyholes.
A fish getting itself entangled in a trap, a woman
Clasps her catch at the carnival of sexes.

While I'm wrapped up in caged lust
Of painted flesh
My thoughts swerve from bared swords to buxom
Amazons in cabaret and brothel.

Straying heroes, crowned or not, will feel regret:
I'm staying home, throw in my lot
With their scorned women who shackle me
To bars or railing of an iron bed.

II

Remember the studio at the Rokin –
An afternoon in the 1940s:

Tubes on the table, you with a cigarette, in your drab suit;
A former stockroom, the attic still reeks of tobacco.

Almost no food. A bit of salt and hardly any bread.
That morning watery gruel made from oats or gravel.

You mutter something, you are often 'übermüdet'                    over-tired
And overcome with sorrow.

We are an hour or so alone;
You have 'cycled herum durch empty Judenstraßen'                  around through
                                                                 empty Jewish streets
And gruffly note: Très déprimé!

(Café 'In 't Kaperschip' always gets you through
With schnaps, to a degree)

Daily you keep journal, measured, very banal.
Pent-up heartache drives your painter's hand.

'Viel gearbeitet, hm hm, erschöpft, na-ja –'                     worked a lot...exhausted
And when the work succeeds: 'Ha Ho – Ha, Ha!'

(Your mouth a thin line that didn't often speak –
Not language, the dream of an imagined space did all the talking.)

III

An old god you are, tormented but untamed –
Surrounded all the time by women
Whom you present repeatedly in awesome shapes.

You lead the dance of brushes, perfect
A pair of earthly legs, smear lustily along a spear,
A table top, a sturdy part of a behind,
While a dark keyhole casually is whitened.

You move as if in a dance hall, clench
A brush between your lips
And fix a young girl's eyes
Who sits capaciously on a too small table.

You exhaust yourself until the light has disappeared
From the depopulated streets.

The last candle, first painted and then lit
Shines in a wet and still unfinished face.

Fate does decide: we stay inside now that the world
Is being darkened and you listen sadly, under this fragile roof,
To the sirens sounding the alarm.

Your sentences trail off; like every night
You travel to never closed-off beaches.

I say, come on, let's have a drink!
Let Quappi come with glasses,
I've brought schnaps and cigarettes along.

We dream away in blue and grey –
Piloted by Greek hands we now doze off
While setting sail to Messingstadt ...

**Notes:**
*Max Beckmann*, German painter, fled from Nazi-Germany to Holland in 1937. Lived in Amsterdam till 1947, emigrated to the U.S. where he died in 1950 while on a walk near Central Park, N.Y. Quappi was the pet name of his wife Mathilde.
*Messingstadt (Brass City)* was painted in Amsterdam, 1944.

From: *Overgangsriten / Rites of Passage*

# The Surrounding and Nearby

1

The first light so close by, so far away
that life is wondering where it will stay.
It once fulfilled itself
under that birch tree, at that window, on the path
to the shed, when it snowed, the door stood ajar
for a while, a boy felled something, the blow of an axe
cut open the milkwhite wood.

2

Awake from night cold behind the window.
Stripped of honey and autumn, the winter
took possession of the eye. The body
evaporated like a nut scent in December.
Was it then that the blue of the berries
blackened, the mud hardened, a snow hare
in whitened grass moved its ears?

3

As long as nothing tapped or sighed, the images that would last
were germinating. While he looked and not looked, sat
at the window, greeted the cold earliness, as ice stood
in the bucket and the wind sometimes abruptly
stroked the ground or sobbed dryly in the hazelnut,
everything exposed itself easily: before his eyes
was the garden of clear death and misty life.

4

Moon white sank into the terrace, shadow images retreated from the
shutters.
First steps around the house, frozen gravel, walkable mud,
old snow between the hedges. Light from light, still
borrowed, without colour, was creeping closer through the bushes.
Forgotten things in the empty yard, a hat, a stick,
a chair by the oak, a doll on a nail. The axe,
recently sharpened, on the block beside the door.

5

Marvels of simplicity existed. That an incinerated
briquette on the grate had kept its shape.
How the dark hermitage in which he lived still made
for a warm sight: the glow in the ashpan, the bed
in the corner, the bread on the table, a teapot, a book.
Remembered silence, never found again. To retain that.
And that the cold had not yet corrupted into a heartless chill.

6

The fire was stirred or rounded up. Powderblack descended
on the hearth stone. To bed, fully clothed, with hot-water bottle
and scarf and papers everywhere against the draft. The wooden
walls creaked, each night a blanket slid to the floor.
There was no difference between in- or outside.
But when he dreamt, it became summer and he was standing,
flustered, beside a dark woman on a dusky forest road.

7

Was this the life that would go on?
Then too villains seized power or weapons
and the world cried out.
But he had to guard what would one day disappear: the garden,
the terrace, the shed in the grass and weathered faces
under the lindens. To be standing there like that, pollarded, ossified
embracing each other with wintry joints.

From: *Een tuin in de winter / A Garden in Winter*

Poems from
*Cantus Firmus, Splendor &*
*Speaking in Tongues*

# Cantus Firmus (a selection)

1

It is autumn or nearly winter,
the painter wants it so, look here.
A *Seelenlandschaft* without people, a hidden country house.
Perhaps an image to inhabit?
    < The land still empty, the soul
yet free >
the panel tells us on the back in faded letters.
    Is it perhaps the kind of house that,
with a longing that could barely be contained, one wanted
to move into all one's life?

Logs lie at the forest's edge
in the axil of two paths –
unsawed loaves, piled high for the new year.

    And just when someone said: 'Hear, hear
the pheasant's call! Carve now the names
into the wood that will be burned tomorrow' –
someone else said something
about an early banquet, a late supper, and that
one had already waited for a century or more
    in the grey mansion with its shutters,
there,
between bare plane trees
on which invariably falls a snowy light –

2

Is this the house that was already there?
before I took a breath? And did she write
a song that as a dreamlike poem
would settle in me?

Or did she not write?

How to approach her? Was I perhaps
a stalker, never letting go, a
hunter in disguise, or the night thief
taking up quarters in her room,
her body wear and daydreams?

Could he regain this way
what I had never owned?

3

Night and a white moon: the silent
lane wears ice crystals and light –

Is there behind the window not some movement?

A man, nearly alien to me
is wandering around the house. Each night
she seems to softly open up a shutter
and then wave at a shadow
who is, as always, breathing down my neck.

What was she hiding then
that he knew nothing of?

4

Yes, to follow once again the traces of a disappearance.
Will ever be fulfilled what keeps on starting here?

Mist on the forest's edge lures me out into the fields.

Look back, no better not to look: the country house
is ruined, with rusty hinges, broken shutters,
stone turned to rubble, wood rot, mould,
        a staircase to the terrace that collapsed.
And she there, yet unbroken
as a vital but elusive goddess
who in tree top, high above the mist,
weaves a dazzling web of light at sunrise.

5

Oh Coleridge, soul-mate, companion! This wintry
house, enclosed by spruce and plane trees
calls 'Frost at midnight' up in me:
    '*The Frost performs its secret ministry,*
*Unhelped by any wind. The owlet's cry*
*Came loud – and hark, again! Loud as before.*'

You knew everything and yet knew nothing.

You didn't know where you should look for her,
or that Asra left you
and cherished colleagues let you down.
    You were 'poor Coleridge', you barely
rose above death's darknesses,
got drunk each day on words, plans, images.
You dazzled and fell, and dazzled again,
captivating and obsessed.
You died of unrequited love;
you swallowed, drank and sniffed
in order to complete the incomplete
once and for all, and fast
while you were still alive.

To numb this futile yearning,
and insatiable desire.

It is midnight again
the moon hangs white and full in the bare planes.
The frost performs its secret ministry.
The owlet cries – 'toowee, toowoo' …

Sister field mouse seeks refuge at my foot.
It will be hours before the roosters crow.

7

Dark eyes and long brown hair, sometimes put up.
The fugitive body is untraceable
in rooms in which she then and recently had been.
A scent (hers unmistakably), a footprint in the dust,
a door that is ajar, draft in an icy hall.
The kettle on the table (scoured and self-repaired), a pencil (but no
note) is all that's left.

The dismantled space, worm-eaten wood, plank
floor, not scrubbed in a long time.
Where once a handbag lay, a book,
her childhood doll,
a rat is feasting
on what whoever
left behind.

10

That she had ever,
that she had on the hearthrug, in the glow
of the stove, said her name to him
and whispered something unintelligible,
while the winter night etched frost flowers on the window
and she for once, for once blossomed open, for once
unfolded herself
and that nobody saw how he lost himself in her
and she took him to her
but had already disappeared
when he stood up from the memory of her embrace
as the inconsolable who seeks infinity.

11

Silently she lived with the seasons
strangely closed like the house that she possessed.

Words buckled, crept away into the seams.

How she hid herself while her body blossomed
and how her spirit chilled and shunned him.

What he regarded as a mystery
turned out to be a void.

And could her face betray something
that the walls had never heard?

15

Her body was a quiet inn out in the countryside.

You rarely saw her out of doors.
She was beauty who cultivated her timidity.

She was the pretty widow who in distant villages
was talked about in taverns.

She veiled her appearance
with shawls and capes.

Her body was a quiet inn out in the countryside.

18  <soggetto cavato>

To lie together one more time beside the fire,
hour after hour, day after day

to stand before the house again
after an instant of a hundred years

the way it was once built.

The day was mild, the evening
brought a mist that was transparent.

Old friends are for the last, for the first
time in that century, expected.

The rooms have been redone, there is
a glow spread by the stove, the rugs

feel warm under our feet.

There has been scrubbing, sanding, papering
of walls; there is a tapestry, a larder.

A choice of wines and dishes
stand on wooden trestles by the wall.

The hour is nearly there. Hushed voices.
Someone pushes the shutters open to the moonlight.

Guests are crowding round the window.
A veil of blue light descends over their faces.

A hundred times friends of the house have stood there.

Someone tinkles with the glasses
and spills wine.

It is the stone guest who behind their backs
starts singing, uninvited.

What he sings is about
money, cyberspace and virtual

matter. He is the master of deception, a mafioso property
developer in a custom-made suit, able to buy or make

or break whatever. With the sledge hammer of his power
he wants to take down moon and stars and

the construction of the mind.

He fobs off people for one night.
Tomorrow he will raze the house among the planes.

What was fragile and in vain like
love is now no longer relevant.

All that has lived here hidden will soon be erased.

From: *Oesters & gestoofde pot / Oysters & Casserole*

# A Gust of Wind in August

What was so special that day
that a gust of wind through the bushes even now
still whispers in your head?
A day in August, a day
like other days, everything had the appearance
of a template, a sloping sand path covered
with crushed tree bark, silence, sunlight,
sweltering heat.
Two small figures on a dune top in the distance.
    You experienced loneliness as unsoluble,
– yes, that cliché too –
and it was for always, if not for eternity (that much was certain).
And that only from yourself you could derive the strength
to endure what life
in the way of truth and brute lies would bring.
Sometimes there was love,
but love proved fleeting and seriously
weakened by betrayal.
    Suddenly the wind went through dwarf birches and dry oak groves –
That was all: a rustling
in silvery light and the wind that touched you, stroked you, persistently,
full of affection it seemed,
as if there was something more than wind
that struck you.
A shiver ran down your back, through your body, everything
was in motion, as if the wind, that strange guest, unexpectedly
entered a heart chamber, then quieted down
and stayed there, did not play up again
or shrank, until it was finally forgotten.
    Today, after forty years – the templates punched
into the marrow of your being – the gust of wind
came suddenly to life again.
A shivering that did not subside passed once more through your body
that was by now a different body.

You were touched again, saw the same bushes
on a walk to sea, the summer sun, the sand path
with its shredded wood. And two
small figures kissing on a dune top in the distance.
You felt how the wind breathed something into you
that you accepted but did not understand.
It did not last a minute while you gave yourself
to wind and shivering and drank in
to the full what the earth was giving.
You knew, you would pay dearly for it all – with something like
a life in service
to something like the word
which had to encompass both birth and death.

It was absolute, but nearly nothing.


From: *Oesters & gestoofde pot / Oysters & Casserole*

# September

The starlings left
before the berries ripened

A blue still flutters among violets
a gauzy gold eye imitates a butterfly

Birches are losing leaves already,
chestnuts explode from sturdy burrs

Hares flee across the fields,
a hunter points his ancient rifle

Pulls the trigger hastily
and puts buckshot in his face

The ferns are withering, dew-
heavy asters droop on bamboo poles

Roses are florishing once more,
buds aren't budging

The buzzard plunges down upon a mouse,
the heron grabs a redeye from a pool

On the land a thresher drones,
a corn field gets de-cobbed

In the distance a delicate haze
hangs over meadow grass –

From: *Splendor*

# Winter Sentence

A grey sky which for hours
    spelled snow
restrained itself, then shyly
sent a scattering of flakes
as a promise for the night
in which you wakefully
lay sleeping, until the dawn
no longer held the snowing back
and you, buzzing with joy,
began the day and from the attic window
surveyed the centuries and the white-dusted fields
beside the country road,
    while nothing broke that rapture –

From: *Splendor*

# On Piazzolla Street

1

Often it's
the placing of objects
on a table
  someone once wrote in a letter.
The drinking glass, the hairpin,
a rose in a bottle,
just sprinkled and given
fresh water.

How you begin
is a question
that matters each time again.
The end yet unknown, the path
never cleared
you follow inborn strategies,
conflicting ideas, pliant
or unbending,
and held together by the rules of a mysterious game.

That you start, time
and again, while you don't matter yourself.
And what it is about
is of less importance than music
in the street, a deserted station, a pain
that permeates life.

Shadow and light fall, lucid
manoeuvres,
feelings about, thoughts of,
sometimes also
an object of friendship, of rapture or hate.

Only seldom now and without illusions
you conjugate
to invoke (invoked, has invoked).

It comes down to
birth and death and in between some love
that lives and passes.
Platitudes that are each time
phrased anew
on a run-down terrace in a backstreet.

Yet each time there are still eyes that shine.
Yours.
You drink in what you've seen and refill the glass.
The end is in sight, the path cleared, a poem
almost done
you know hardly anything matters.

You are sailing on a damaged planet
through ill-fated and indifferent space.

2

'Where to start,' someone wrote you
   in a letter.
Often it's close by:
an animal along the road (the armadillo
that was crossing blindly), a landscape, a fox
on the barn, a sparrow
in the hedge, an empty house
at the edge of a wood – a downpour
lashing the plane trees.

Or perhaps a hare
riddling a sleeping
hunter with gunshot.

Or as here,
glued together, eyes half closed,
   a tango-dancing pair
on the corner of a street at night.
The bar badly lit, plastic chairs
   on an empty sidewalk.
He, wrinkled and earnest, in old jacket and hat
a silk scarf around his neck.
She, a ruined beauty
   in a tight dress with a slit
who somewhat slowly, as in passing,
has just accomplished a swing of the leg
with finesse:
Raw and intimate this dance
a poem
that with casual mastery
leaves everything else behind.

3

This hole in the wall, a dump beyond redemption:

*Perro* with mange at the door, a rundown
cantina, people living
on the doorstep with absinth, bile-green
paint on the wall
flaking into the glasses.
How Felipe is sucked off behind the counter
and Mary Jane has her pussy eaten on a table –
Backpacker from the U.S., stranded
here one day
   when a tango abruptly
bit into her soul.
And no one dancing or drinking
can foresee
that the lovers, like mangy dogs,
will only get to the end of the film
of the book
– ripened by experience, struck dumb by grief –
in cruel isolation.

Mary Jane Reed: *Selfportrait, or
What a Sexy Tango Did to Me.*

4

The physical universe
   of a tango-dancing pair –

Tango is Tao:
banned chaos
nature subdued.

This is how it starts again every night:
The bodies are slightly apart
      and yet inextricably
entwined.
The man in the old jacket,
the woman with a rose in the dyed-black hair
   move sternly and daringly
through the light
on the corner of a seedy street.

Music sucks the dirt
from invisible wounds.
Restrained love breaks out
from the hole in the wall.

The shoes shine as ever.
Shoes are the pride and dignity
   of those who hardly own anything.
This dance a closed domain.
A body-to-body on the road to oblivion.
Elsewhere a home altar waits
with plastic flowers and the smile of the Holy Virgin.
A heavenly hour equal to Her
   and yet to be of mortal flesh.
Rarely fit, forever tired, not yet
gone under from life
they wheel with measured steps through the night.

Deep chant. Bandoneón.
It ends with the body and the earth.
It ends in the quarter, the street, the bar.
Bitterness and sadness in the heart.
   *El cuerpo y la tierra*
Bitterness sweetened by pain.
*¡La calle Piazzolla en mi corazón!*

From: *Het vertrapte mysterie / The Trampled Mystery*

## Time Is

You want to catch the present
while it no longer exists.
Time is a passage, a closed
counter, where you're always too late –

Time is the equalizer.
Time heals nothing, but inflicts
new wounds. What comes into flower
will be decomposed by it.

Time is deeply rooted, smells of the seasons.
A scent thins out, a month slips by.
It settles in manure and fruit, a rose bush, chestnut leaves.
Time lives in a summer past, sea air, remembered girl's hair.
It hides in baby balm, spent love, a ravaged skin.

Time is a snail at breakneck speed. For children
slowly passing, nothing stops its course
till you're lying on a bier at the edge of bittersweet waters.

# Three Metamorphoses

## En Toute Candeur
*Myrrha's fate*

That his gaze from the beginning took my breath away,
Made me afraid of death and sick of life.

Nothing held me back, she said,
Nothing could have stopped me:
*Where the love, there the eye.*

As if the words themselves bolstered her senses,
And she that night struck him with blindness,
At the place where she was standing then
Brought him with date wine and sweet scents to ecstasy.
And how she standing where she stood
Was lost and he who drank
Absorbed her and defiled her irreparably.

That he more than once that night
Refound himself in me, she said
Bestowed shudderings of triumph –
Until he, yet before the break of day
Made light and saw me in all innocence.

The ground gave way under my feet.
How murderous rage chased lust away,
How he drove me off,
And I, unclothed, fled in great haste,
Losing my face; dragging myself along, forever slower, heavier,
Soon without hands, my skin already wooden, the toes (with roots)
Digging themselves into the earth.

In short, the story of a flight that gets bogged down.

And that since then something grows deep inside me,
A fruit, still unborn and unwritten, something
Adorable perhaps, a redeemed desire
That in the twilight of my body
Unfolds, nearly breaks me
As I forever deeper root into the earth.

No father who will catch my tears
Nor smell the blood track of his fallen angel.

Ovid, *Metamorphoses*, X, 298-518

## The Enchanted Ship
The adventures of Acoetes, told by himself to Pentheus the Cruel


Not to Naxos?
Naxos lay elsewhere and behind us.
The islands came no closer.

A kidnapped boy, the sleepy haul
     of greedy mates.
Derisive laughter when I said:
'There is a god in him,
Though I do not know which god.'

The sun spilled light upon the water.
And I, Acoetes, stood there, and the god
Stood there beside me, the aftertaste
     of must still on his tongue.
Both languid, in the languid
     sun-baked afternoon
Below the coast, before the foaming cliff,
On the slow undulation –
     The heads red and light-sated,
The eyes directed at something that didn't come.
And the mutinous rowers held the oars upright,
Like air riders, like air rowers,
(Lycabas, the Lydian, beat me yet into the rigging).
Oars heavy, suddenly entwined; vines
Tied themselves around the rudder, around the mast;
     From the deck veiled growth shot up,
A rioting of tendrils, ivy and lianas
Entangling the ship's rump, raised
From the shining by an unseen hand.
     The anchor thick with dripping leaves.
The ropes, the battens,
The seats cloaked with green garlands.
Panthers and lynxes flanked the god.

The fish-tailed sailors growing scales, huddled
Together, beaten and defeated; then toppled
Overboard.
Dolphins making water music, somersaulting,
     foam splashing on the snouts,
All tumbling mutineers,
Except me, Acoetes, skipper and slave
Who, sailing to Naxos,
Honoured the god with the wine-red lips.

Ovid, *Metamorphoses*, III, 572-691

# Kingfisher at Sea

Spellbound in Morpheus' arms
She saw her husband, drowned,
Stand there in sodden clothes

She hastened to the beach
No one prevented her
Day broke, the storm died down

She saw a body floating out at sea
It had the shirt and hair
The figure of her spouse

She swayed and wailed
(Her mouth turning into a beak)
Running along the tide line

She swayed and wailed
Skimmed low over a levee
Up to the water

Broken waves at her feet
A mutilated body thrown onto the rocks
The gods speaking winged language

Once again she rushed towards him
Who for some time had appeared
To her at night

How the gods were slowing down her wingbeat
Until the dead man rose again and he
With Alcyone chose the windless air

Ovid, *Metamorphoses* XI, 410-748

# The Great Disdain
*a fable*

1

Raven possessed little of worth:
a flashlight, a dungheap, a dirty feather suit.

It was dark and empty on earth.

What he wanted to see, he had to make:
a bird, a human, a woman who could
give birth, a maple, a sea bass
with jaws, a lobster swimming
around with deadly claws.

Raven didn't want to learn anything.
He had no memory and barely a brain.
You had to guess his gender, his thieving paw
became a girl's hand if required. The shack
in which he lived had Neverthought as its name.

2

Before the daylight
beheld the daylight
it was found as a glowing ball
between rubbish, filthy bones,
old toys and all.
Whatever lay on the ground he would kick
(he always thought that was cool).
Raven kicked so hard that the fire ball
flew up and escaped through the smoke hole.

That's how the light came to earth –

after which, full of himself,
he married his mirror image
in a muddy pool.

3

He sat beside his image on a branch
in a tree he had created first.
Raven shit, three feet high around the trunk
was the fare he stuffed his face with.

4

Raven was jealous. His gluttony
knew no bounds.
He spied on humans and gave them
hell, beat some of them to death
before he was beaten himself.
He ate from the flesh, burped for two
and had only just sat down
on the corpse catching his breath
   when he fancied another bite
for it had, he said,
the perfect rat taste of a Big Mac.

Raven spat and deceived,
shrugged at all
that lived, breathed,
sang or stirred.
Nothing ever disturbed his sleep.

Raven had no views,
he murdered, stole and stuffed his face,
   'that's how I shake off everything!' he croaked.
'My preference is for
a nutricous diet with a lot of meat!'

It went the way it goes.
It was the usual deal.

5

There was always something hanging over his head:
A splitting axe. A carving knife.
Sometimes a pipe of lead.

When he was caught
they would break his paw, singe
his feather pack and shave
him bald. His nose was glued
to his back, he was hung
and after that hacked into bits.

The higher he climbed, the lower he fell.
But, when it came to the crunch,
his slyness always helped him out.

Raven wailed, screamed, melted
hearts, played the part of a dunce
or performed
as the Man of Unbearable Woe.

He arose from the dead, now thin
as a rake, swore revenge
by the excreta of snakes
and immediately burrowed for maggots,
worms and bait
that was in a state of decomposition.
Never again would someone
get the better of him, or the dogs
have him for lunch.

6

He made a power grab:
The animals of democracy were
– with cheers from a packed house –
raped in the raven arena,
where a thousand cameras openly
recorded every detail of his act.

Instantly Raven was
a great man, a true popular
tyrant whose stupidity
enthralled everyone in the land.
His appearance and proclamation
of the Raven doctrine
were repeated day and night on every screen.

The great disdain in him grew.

7

Raven was an idol of the people,
that he had modelled after himself.

He rasped: 'Decency is undoable!'
And: 'My deeds will set things right!

His voice was praised,
they heard bel canto, how he could sing!
'Croak-croak! I am the world,
the earth can't teach me anything!'

Raven had a lot to do.
All that had been made
he now had to undo.

A child could see
that he paired the evil eye
with delusion and spite.

8

Then one day
without mercy
he shot the sun to smithereens
like a pidgeon of clay.

The light in the sky went out,
no vistas could be seen.

Raven wondered
how this could be.
He spat on the ground and flew off
his feathers askew.

The ink-black space
closed around him for good.

Everything withered, grew rigid and died.
Maggots and worms also froze underfoot.

The earth was dark and empty again.


[2003]


From: *Het vertrapte mysterie* / *The Trampled Mystery*


97

# Nansen on the Ice Sea

After two years in pack ice on the *Fram*
Nansen and his companion departed
March 1895
  with three sledges,
  eighteen dogs,
  skis and two kayaks
in the direction of the Pole,
while the ship and her crew drifted,
slower than slow, towards unknown horizons.

Parkas, iPhones, snowmobiles
and ski-planes were unknown.
Johansen and Nansen wore reindeer shoes
warmed by sedge grass.
Clothing was thawed out and dried on the body.
The mercury froze; fingers were white
and numb when they woke up in the tent.
  Slowly it went northward,
a long slog was sometimes cancelled out
when the ice moved southward, imperceptibly.

Nine-feet-high ice walls sapped the strength of dogs and men,
sledges got caught behind ice floes, breaking up
in the early Spring sun.
Strung together the kayaks could
carry a number of dogs on two sledges.
  The days lengthened
  and did not turn into night.
The animals whined, paws covered with sores;
the men, plodding like beetles in loose sand,
looked for and found a way in blinding emptiness.

On April 8th they stood at less
  than four degrees from the Pole –
  a last spurt seemed obvious.
Resolutely, perhaps with regret, they
cool-headedly turned around: the North Pole
  wasn't worth death by starvation and posthumous fame.

The expanse of ice drifted in unknown directions.

Until the end of June no bear or seal
  or bird of prey was seen.
The daily food scarce, out of necessity
they shot the dogs that summer.
Franz Josef Land – iced-in archipelago – appeared in August.
Only after days it lay within their reach.
Wintering over on the coast crept closer.

Food and life returned:
bears and walruses offered themselves,
a Ross-gull zoomed past
and climbed on the wind high in the sky.
  First a cave for shelter, then
  a tight abode put up from boulders, moss
  and walrus skins,
  large enough to lie stretched out in.
  Blubber lamps brought light, relief
  and seared up small wounds.
The sun went into hiding; halfway
October a months-long night began.
The bears dozed off, the men slept also
when they weren't eating.

Provisions for the winter were stored on the roof.

A bitterly cold Christmas brought a sense
   of insignificance and intense loneliness.
'A frightening silence,' even grabbed Nansen by the throat.
He wrote: 'Here is already the great emptiness
that will reign on earth when it wheels dead
and barren through immeasurable space.'

The new year started with a bright moon
and forty degrees below,
Euphoric, they walked back and forth on the snowy rocks,
underwent in the moonlight the power and beauty
   of a cosmic tableau.
A glacier fired shots of joy in the blue night.

Frithjof and Hjalmar wore rags stuck to the skin,
that started bleeding when some threadbare cloth was loosened.
Hair, beard for months already black from oil and dirt:
blubber and meat there was aplenty.
   But the foxes turned out
   to be master thieves.

May '96: the winter quarters were abandoned.
Nansen hung a tube with notes on paper
at the entrance of the hut.
   The kayaks put on sleds held all they needed to survive.
The further on they went, the more brittle the ice.
The softer the snow, the more often a splitting slab
turned quickly into open water.

Unexpectedly disaster struck: the kayaks – moored and pinned down – slipped off a porous edge and drifted rapidly away. Nansen jumped fully clothed into the sea and swam after them. Although overcome by cold and ice water, he got hold of the two and in addition grabbed his gun and managed to shoot two birds on the point of a kayak … Hoisted onto the ice by his mate, his clothes were pulled off his body and not much later he lay shivering under the tent roof in the sleeping bag, eating soup with bird meat.

After a journey on foot over fibrous ice, in the middle of June they heard dogs barking. Shortly afterwards they ran into an Englishman. It was the Pole explorer Frederick Jackson who had already spent two years in the High North. After some hesitation he saw who one of the wild-looking, filthy men was.

'Aren't you Nansen?'
'Yes, I am.'
'By Jupiter, I am glad to see you!' Jackson exclaimed.
And pulled out letters from his bag for the Norwegians.

The steamer Windward brought them home in August.

From: *In tongen spreken / Speaking in Tongues*

# Whip-Shaped Sermon

*Aaah!*
♫♪♫♪ Sing! ♫♪♫♪
Or hang yourself! †††
Be thrown like Jonah on an empty coast.
Plumb the mystery, descend
into the earth. Swallow
disgust, alleviate
the pain, not the hunger
for a tempestuous love. Grow
underground. Let your thoughts
branch out invisibly. Be
subversive and grotesque. Emerge
and disappear, undermine
the vicious power of banking
worms, sow panic among weasels
& jackals of the stock exchange. Gnaw
at the fibres of communication.
Tackle and slash the force
that doesn't unite but uniformizes.

Entrap stupidity
in its own nets. Deal also
firmly with yourself. Trample
hypocrisy. Reject
and despise: better to choose
the lasting horror of clausura
(no scanty friendship, no dislodged
trust).
Time postpones itself each day,
a joint that smoothly turns
or balefully creaks.
Its lust to gobble up is seen as
wastefulness. Therefore live
a life that's not watered down by others.

What affects you to the core
    is that you want it all and contrive nothing.
   Be pliant like bamboo, elusive like the wind.
  Witness all things, don't break yet.
Put a cordon of words around the present.
       Yell!
       Erupt
       In un-
       Ashamed
       Laughter

        ▲
        ▲
        ▲
        ▲
        ▲

From: *Hollandse Sermoenen / Dutch Sermons*

# Introverted Sermon

*'... we could not consort*
*with each other nor could we consort with me.'* (Leonard Nolens)


Now that man, roughly speaking,
has been promoted to offal again,
we turn inward
and turn away –

to till the blood red earth again,
fill the barns,
empty the glasses,
build a house without fear.

Time is a construct,
so the agreement goes.
    What has happened
     has not happened
(after all we have to live).

The present does not exist,
the truth is constantly overtaken,
the raging dead push each other aside.

Who fools around with the prophet dies by the sword.
Who loves his enemy will be sorry.

The present worms itself each moment
like an impertinent guest
between what was
and what's ahead of us.

'It is then. It is this. It is soon.'

What has been done
reminds us
of what we still want:

Intensify the yearning,
clothe desire with
scantily covered flesh,
tangible,

sometimes unsparing
like the minimal gesture
that betrays intimate promises.

Was it then. Will it be this. Will it be soon

when you shrink,
and rolled up
'like a larva in the frosty night light'
without a hat, by waxing moon,
with a clouded mind
are swept up
and done away with

heading towards a cold destiny?

Don't worry too much
about words
that will easily bear other ones –
never intentionally
but moulded the way they came:
    Without adornment, in a hair shirt
even, risen up from pure joy
first from mouth and throat,
    written down,
descended once again through eye and ear
and here, at this moment,
on this page
in trust passed on
to that one reader.

# Sermon for Deaf Ears

1

A sermon like a three-piece suit
that does not fit,
that's not quite tailor-made
and refuses to conform
to the latest trend –

Take back the word taken from you.
Move your tongue, erupt, stand out,
    speak to those turning a deaf ear.
Sing on if nothing works, richly, in tune,
even when unanswered.

Be the fool in the bushes,
play Tourette in the street.

2

Neither townsfolk nor trees, birds nor fishes
understood the miraculous tales –
    the lotus sutra
    the sermon of enlightenment
    the conversation under a straw roof.
    The exemplum. The *setsuwa*. The exemplary story.

The situation became unbearable –

Geese howled, piglets screamed,
carp shot like dolphins through the ditch.
The farmer, he ploughed
stolidly through the words,
let the tractor rage on, driverless
    during heathen lunch breaks
    with a strapping daughter of the land.

You drew furrows through his brain
inducing him in vain to diesel silence.
Laughter and scorn: bleating beer-drinking locals
pushing forward. The stone crusher was deployed,
here a mower, there a sledge hammer was tried out. A chainsaw
    cutting up culled pig bones, a horror song
    cancelled out winged uproar in the branches.

The situation was critical –

Neither townsfolk nor trees, birds nor fishes
were spared.
No one still understood the miraculous tales –
    the lotus sutra
    the sermon of enlightenment, the book
    of the way and its power, the sound of stealthy rain
    with which a happy melancholy is greeted.

Delight is the word.
That the identical twins of heaven and hell
delight time and again in
what prevents us from living.
        And you, imbued with the nearby
        behold the Pole Star in dark hours...

**Note:**
The third part of this 'three-piece' sermon has been omitted because of its length. It deals
with Jacques de Vitry – a medieval celebrity of the Church, involved in crusades against
Cathars and Saracens – who wrote 74 'exemplary' sermons. Self-mockingly the poet calls
himself Vitry's 'heretical descendant' and 'perverted heir'.

# What I Saw and Underwent

What I saw and underwent
was to my liking:
not only did it please me,
I was struck
by something blank,
a whiplash of enormous force
something from on high
which was dark, anonymous and nondescript.
It landed
like unforeseen violence.
I just survived it, proved
unable to resist a rapture
without equal.
I thought of all those lives
that never endured it.
When I came to my senses
and regarded it up close,
now step by step, frightened as well,
made it my own,
it began to pall on me,
I renounced it,
I began to hate it.
The aversion became so great
that I embraced it out of spite
and tried to understand it
in a language
that did justice
to what I just now rejected
(but was excellent in every way)
and did not betray myself
or my sincerity.
It started to grow in me
the way I had grown in all
I had seen and undergone,

so that it enfolded itself
and came to full development.
It lit up,
it flamed high;
a heavenly fire did not let go of me.
I then bowed before its splendour
and the dark force
with which it kept me under control
and subjected me to hellish tortures that were also sweet.
Its roughness was a blessing,
and I loved its stranglehold.
While it nearly smothered me
it, in turn, drank in
my undivided attention.
Breathlessly I looked at it
and felt how my gaze
was mirrored in something
that seemed to be dark glass.
We found ourselves in a pleasant
and acute distress.
I now knew
it demanded everything from us,
and imposed for an indefinite duration
a hardly human
toll on me.
Before it was absorbed in me
and let itself be merged
I tasted the only absolute
that's left to us;
that will be completed
in the hour of our death.

From: *Hollandse Sermoenen / Dutch Sermons*

# Five Dances of Death

## In the Year of the Plague
*je fis de macabree la danse*

I think it happened in 1348:
a thousand vagabonds
blind drunk like lice en route to Kolenberg.
Although watched and enclosed
by a sweet yellow smell, we stalked the women –
severely sloshed and seduced by fish sauce of Saint George,
cramps broke loose from the alcoves
and the butt-fox who blew her three times
in the ass won the prize –
a fat capon, a token of regard from Quackadore.

What did we know about views
of an old castle, there was mud
on the wrappings and a free grave from where
the wind passed on its sickly spoils
to doctors and to goliards,
to the drinkers on the ship of fools.

When I was old
love's illness felled me
once and for all.

A misunderstanding: again you find yourself at the beginning
(worn-out, betrayed, still wet from birth)
and know too much. There are taverns,
sounds in the distance, the same sun
shines, but on a different elder tree.
And that the days are coming to an end.

You wander, look around,
cough like before and feel the cold.
What was once called colony
is now the front;
for the rest they keep devouring each other, couth and uncouth
with skin and all. And with imagination on the wane
the gentlemen you meet are really clerks
with a small defect
whose greed & lies
are as always tactfully concealed.

The trembling of my hand is permanent,
infected, you don't lick sores.
What's left is looking in the sun,
blowing a cloud of smoke and wondering
if ever it could have been otherwise.


[1964]

**Note:**
'Kolenberg' was the unofficial name for the shady part of a town where wanderers and
drifters of all stripes would come together to spend the winter. A kind of sanctuary.


From: *Poolsneeuw / Polar Snow*

# Lübeck

*'Ik schal dansen unde kan nit gân.'*        *'I will dance and cannot go.'*

Too late for Travemünde,
Body, map and time
Have slowly become chains,
Words do react to one another,
The matter can't be disentangled
As it encloses me and eats away at me.

I travel back and had
Moved in with Lotte Förster.
Skin-over-bones with human face;
Shortly before – a tackle in the bushes,
A third degree and whip lash on the neck –
It looked like I was done for.

My book of hours I gave her,
She took off her ring and hennin.        *headdress*
I then gave her my dagger
Though it was winter.
The grass widow thus snared the butt fox
With his begging bowl.

Late lover, callow still, my throat
All acid and peppers –
She said: *was du bist das was ich*,       *What you are I was once*
Unknowing, full of life.
She smelled her spouse in me
Who sailed with wine and silk at the Cyclades.

Through centuries I see her humane face
Next to my withered mug.
It begins to snow, in winter
Time and town bogged down.
Boils started branching out
Into furtive tooth decay.

Later it turned out, she liked down under
In church portals. I joined her, playing
Brother Lollaard with his Lute, for
She served, so to speak, gods with her ass.
When I moved on again
She'd caught a dose from me.


[1965]

**Notes:**
*Lübeck* was known for its 'dance of death', carved in wood on a tomb in the Church of St. Mary.
*Travemünde*: harbour near Lübeck where the ferry to Sweden departs.
*Lollaards and Lutes* (beguines named after Lutgardis) were wandering people belonging to a
fake religious order, who were, just like the more educated Goliards, part of a so-called *ordo
vagorum*. They only revered the 'god' of prostitution, cheating and adultery.


From: *Swartkrans / Swartkrans*

## Dança Mortal

I had wanted to hunt partridges
before the day was done.

The empty village square lies trembling in the sun

I played here in my younger years
and merrily walk down the green.

An ambush suddenly: surrounded
by high voices like a hedge

I stand transfixed, my feet nailed to the ground –

In an instant I'm disarmed
by children.

The circle goes round in a song
and helplessly I'm counted out:

> *One is your skirt of water*
> *Two is your bodice of bread*
> *Three is for eating you later*
> *Four is your hands are all red*
>
> *Five 'n six and no one cares*
> *Settle down and say your prayers*
> *For you are dead!*

Heat soils the body, skin turns
to lead in the afternoon sun.

Flies give the eye-sockets of a cadaver
a coppery sheen.

It's already later than I thought:

I had wanted to hunt partridges
before the day was done.


(1977)

From: *Va-banque / All or Nothing*

## Dancemaster Death
(Lübeck 2)


Eastward the plains,
Westward the sea.
Horesemen at the borders,
Ships run aground in flight.
Fra Pole Artick blows the ice wind
Over the land; a whip catches

Blackening flesh. Cold eats
Away at hides and houses.
Thus the winter gets us
In its grip again.
The lice crawl deeper
Into hair.

Tender temptations lure me
Inside the walls
Where wood fires smoke
And bread burns on the grate.
'*O vrou, mit di ik danssen beghinne*' –       '*Oh, woman with you I start to dance*'
Between fish, skinned hares and quails

You are no princess anymore
But a nameless creature
Who in the glow of the last pleasure
Forgot the final hour.
I peddle everything here, bear
On my back the wares of death.

You say: *Ik wuste nicht dattu hir werst.*       *I didn't know that you were here*
I take your hand: you could have known.
See the choral dance that's leaving town,
Hear the starving customer who smells
The bread and knocks, but shuddering
Takes to his heels.

Inside: extinguished fires
And stiffened bodies.
The terror reign of cold and fever.
Outside: sable and hoof beats,
Faraway horsemen hurrying eastward
Through a grey dawn.


[2013]

From: *Kerven, kastijdingen / Nicks & Castigations*

## The Hour Glass

Never a dancer
        of tango or twist
you looked like death out of Lübeck, Ypres, Berlin,
wrote a friend from days gone by.
Everything was said, the last questions
        were not eluded either.
What did we amount to? Less than nothing
we were in spite of that not all that bad.
        Imagination brought us the idea
of un-becoming, clear word
that proved impossible to grasp.

We imagined
the living growing rigid, while death
was already on its way, out of the church,
up the street, into the bar,
where guests and revellers like young dogs
drank to hardcore partying,
danced body to body
and blissed out became entwined with one another.
Fleshy lips sucked ears, mouths, nipples.
Life should be celebrated
  and the barrel emptied.

It was over, the last call
had already sounded, the hour glass
was running out.

High time to depart.

Still kissing they were stripped of flesh
and done away with, sinking first into deep sleep,
then waking as crestfallen skeletons

in a close dance with death.


[2016]

From: *Splendor*

# I Fly through the Thirteenth Century

ABYSSUS ABYSSUM INVOCAT (JOHANNES TAULER)

Sailing over marsh and waste land, the quicksand of the soul
that unnamed and unknown in all its nakedness
awaits the fire of salvation & seduction,
　　the meagre language of mysticism
　　shines over my thinly clothed bones.

*Wüstenunge.* Emptiness. Abyss.

Nothing.

The dark of night brings *vremedunge*
even though Love is all.
Who falls out of the godhead is irrevocably estranged.

A single spark ignites the fallow of the soul.
Divine light streaming out
in Magdeburg, Sint-Truyen, Ypres, Engelthal.
Marie d'Oignies enjoys the reverence of Jacques de Vitry.
She cuts into her flesh and gives her friend
a small slice of her thigh as an amulet or relic on his travels
to ward off bodily harm. Who touches her locks
will be healed on the spot.

The bleeding heart of Christ arouses intense heartbreak
with the women of the free spirit.
The *minnegrif in daz hertz* is a fact. 'Drink, love
the wounds and the delights that are my body.'
　　In Medingen and Engelthal *lüten rüefe* rise. ·
Margareta Ebner shrieks or doesn't say a word
for months sometimes, lies three years paralyzed
in bed, clenches her teeth as if she's catatonic
and then she unexpectedly speaks in tongues,

erupts in a wondrous language of monotonous cries
that she repeats a hundred times.
She scrupulously notes what's wrong with her:
'An arrow full of venom splits my heart, a fist
is pummelling my insides into smithereens.'
Tormented by 'noble desire & insatiable yearning'
she swells up 'like a pregnant woman'
until the Man of Sorrows 'like a friend after the matins'
stands before her in all his nude simplicity
and they exchange their hearts, she kisses him, goes into rapture.
The full jugs of her bosom brush
over the wounds of his emaciated body.

Time of extremes, of trembling and orgasmic
rapture, self-castigation, fasting and humility,
and often too intolerable suffering.
    What the north allows, is cut off by the south.
For three years Domna Prous Boneta stands before her judges    mulier sancta
and is then killed in Montpellier by bigwigs of the church.
Beheaded, burned alive – whichever their decision.

For seven years Christina von Hane fights in the Rhineland
against the seven hellish sins, mostly the one of sensuality.
She tames her sex urge with her harsh asceticism, does penance,
shrieks and withers and writes.
She attacks 'that filthy lust' and mutilates her burning sex
    with lime and vinegar, the glow of a burning branch.
Then, at her wits end, cuts off her clit and labia –
having entered the convent at six, she dies when she is twenty-three.
A perfect soul, they said, who often was with God,
with whom she merged and secretly shared
her life in mindless passion.

The body: image of the soul,
the inner grief externalized.
A true friend of God trembles and glows when his lord
takes shape and unexpectedly appears.
   For Beatrice of Nazareth it feels 'as if her veins
are bursting, the blood dissolves and marrow dries up,
bones are softening, the heart's on fire, the throat
becoming parched, the whole body passing through
this inner heat and fever of love'.                                    furor amoris
Beatrice, who is fighting pain with pain,
wears a girdle made of thorns under her habit.
That what she writes is first inscribed on wax
and then, by copyists with a goose quill,
put onto paper.

In Sint-Truyen Christina is causing a stir.
She's called The Astonishing, floats in the air
and flies to spires and tops of trees,
rolls like a hoop, in prayer, down the street.
She crawls into a burning oven, submerges herself
in boiling water and in Liège she bathes sometimes
for days under the ice of the wintry Meuse.
   Christina is admired and feared, spends weeks
in the cooler where festering abscesses plague her.
Beguine nor nun, the untamed woman
is acknowledged as a fool, because of Christ.
She presses oil from both her breasts
that cures her boils and her eczema.

And twice the winged virgin dies before she really dies.
She cannot bear the air of sin and wicked people.
Surrounded, ogled by devout Sint-Truyen folk and frightened
farmers from the district, some trendy Liège lads,
she lies, not twenty yet, in public on her bier.
She is a sight indeed, even in days to come:

her skin remains intact, no putrefaction and no maggots.
She travels through a different world, visits
the carousel of heaven, hell and purgatory,
withstands a death sleep of six weeks, is
penitent then and hysterical: a female shaman
who isn't recognized as such.
   Christina regains her senses just in time, climbs nimbly
from her coffin, then floats above the convent graves, becomes
intoxicated by her wild exploits.

The overwhelming God pours out his love and light
in her, with the honey flowing
from her sex, which drives her to audacious feats.
   People don't know if she's a ghost
or someone real, her biographer writes.
They peek out from their hovels at the woman
who floats by singing through the vile and pissed-on street.
A nightingale hides in her throat and from its depths
she lets her songs reverberate, sings
in never before heard harmonies, is overwhelmed
by bliss & extasy.                               iubilus
Dogs nibble at her bones; she suffers
epileptic seizures, tumbles down, gets up again.
Driven by divine insanity
she rants and raves until her real death.
Not hurt by anything she's never burned or scratched.
Isn't that miraculous?
   Since she forsakes the world
heaven has become her earth
that she explores perplexed as woman in the woods.
Christina shares her flesh with man and beast.
(Nick Cave sang about her
in a song of little worth.)

Jacques de Vitry lists their names and Cantimpré describes
their lives from first or second-hand accounts.
A sister is called beguina, papelarda, humiliata or bizoche.
Vitry gets a finger of Marie d'Oignies after her death,
Thomas of Cantimpré does not possess a relic from his friend
and peer Lutgardis from the Nivelle diocese.
   It is a time of dogged abstinence and trembling delight.
One looks for love, the light and starves oneself,
passion is the 'maelstrom of the heart'.
One speaks of God as 'the living bread'.
Love is *amor* and *a-mor* equals 'without death'.          'die amorose' of St. Adelwip

Margareta of Ypres, unstable and retiring, not
yet twenty, loves Siger of Rijssel – her counsellor
and friend – as much as The Crucified One.
When asked, Christ lets her know
that her love for Siger
does not corrupt a heavenly marriage.
   Mechthild of Magdeburg, marked by a 'sinking humility'
longs naked in her cell for a night with the only God.
Shaking out her straw bedroll, she mutters a mantra to herself
a thousand times:
   The deeper I sink
   the sweeter I drink,
   the deeper I sink
   the sweeter I drink …
and calls herself in his fleeting light
an eager bride in God's bed

KARISSIMA!
Heavens, now what?
A third Christina appears!
Named Bruso, born in Stommeln, Westphalia.
Has a Swedish friend who, in a fatherly way,
   restrains & loves her.
Petrus of Dacia walks from Stommeln to Paris, studies
with Thomas Aquinas and goes back again on foot
and continues to Gotland, his home.
*Caro, carior, carissimo!*
He is her dearest, that's how she addresses him,
they talk on a grassy berm in the apple yard.
Tears, when they part, deep love
that grows ever more rampant.
Conversations described and letters
   miraculously saved.
'Karissima,' he writes, 'you are also my dearest
whom I yield to, embrace and caress in Christ.'
   She revels in commotion, bustle and the threat of evil.
Demons cut her to pieces (*Zerstückelung* a fact),
but angels restore her body.
Besieged by devils, smeared with muck,
stricken with bleeding wounds during Holy Week
she serves love, madness and God.
Driven from the convent
she returns as farmer's daughter.
Fixes up the old farmstead in a furious rage:
piles up peat, makes a fire, bread on a plate
baked above whispering flames.
She goes to sleep with the beasts, plants rye, milks
goats & scrubs the tiles around the stove,
floats often like an aerial ghost
free as a bird above the land,
and is – thank God – visited by pious monks.

The little ice-age has the farmstead in its grip. Mud
frozen, fields in a deep freeze, rock-hard ground. A hole
in the ice of the ditch for edible animals and mangy dogs.
Snow into April chastises the hares and vagrants
along deserted pilgrim roads.
Inside the house and in her head it sometimes rages.
The biting wind and the cutting cold penetrate
the bitterly-cold box-bed and the drafty animal shed.
It will never be spring again.
    When Petrus dies in Sweden the shutters
to the world are locked until her death.
(After six hundred years and not without hesitation.
Christina Bruso is beatified
by God's stand-in.)


I fly the century out again and land in Engelthal.
Oh Adelheid! I've saved you for the last,
buried deep in a warm stable you lie there with the beasts
in a fertile Bavarian convent vale.
Let me be your counselor and guide.
Oh Adelheid, you are mine and I am yours!
You are quickly disconcerted, even faint          'sī kam so gar von ir selben'
when Christ says: 'My treasure, my beauty, yes
my sugar-sweet love, my mouth tastes
the honey from underneath your tongue.'
    Plump under the coarse brown habit of a nun
that you have rolled up high,
you lie there waiting in the straw.
Oh, Langmann Adelheid, I nearly lose my cool!
You are so hot and round,
You do not fit in a convent cell.
With thighs so firm and hips so broad you lie there
in your too tight skin and wait like Danaë
for golden rain.
As the free spirit that you are
you shouldn't be in here!

'I know what happens,' whispers Mechthild from the side.
'When a heavenly beast he is a delight
like he was with me: come on, she gives herself
to him, that pious girl, he gives himself to her,
and thus they make a perfect pair
and that pleases me indeed.

If you want to understand my words, just read
*The Flowing Light of the Divinity* nine times.'

From: *Splendor*

# Amstel Station 7.1.76 / 9:15

I was struck by you again
in the departing train.

There is no likeness,
a screen of words
hides you from view.

Although you woke me up and shadowed
me for twenty years
you always managed to remain unseen.

Just what you wrote in letters
we were allowed to know of you:

'I am damaged
and bitten
but alive'

You wrote,
   'The sap
will soon surge through the branches'

You super-holy woman,
you are part
of everything I write.

Always the gallows' candidate of theologians
you sometimes got a shape
never a body.


Much talked about and yet
a blank, only as text body
you remained intact.

I read love and seasons
from the furrowed structure of your skin.

Winter went on for centuries, cold
did not eat away at you –

What was a struggle for existence
has become survival art.

Times are still bleak and we already
damaged from before the primal scream.

In a haze of love and pain
your songs keep going through my mind.

Now that I touch you with my eyes
I see again
that glow of dark word glaze.

This poem is dedicated to the mystic poet Hadewijch, who lived in The Southern Nether-
lands (first half of the 13th century). She wrote Visions, Letters and 45 powerful Strophic
Poems. Nothing is known about her.

From: *Nieuwe gedichten / New Poems*

# Arnout of Riberac Sees His Forbidden Love from Afar

Whenever I think of you
    the longing intensifies
to become desire
    that scorches the body and is yet not fulfilled

Whenever you think of me
    your longing intensifies
to become desire
    that once but by a hairbreadth was fulfilled

When we are dizzy with longing
    and not know how
we excessively desire each other and that
    your blood will never merge with mine

we must until the Day of Judgement
    in painful solitude
do without the glow of love
    and body consolation –

Your absence is bringing me to ruin,
    when you suffer my body also hurts.
Ashen I reach for your forbidden form.
    Oh Lady of Bezèrs –

Arnout is bleeding dry from numerous wounds.

From: *In tongen spreken / Speaking in Tongues*

# Splendor
*or*
*the metaphysics of light*


1


From the darkness of November to the beauty of the light.
Not just light, the drinker of the light tastes hues
and nuances as with wines. The senses sharpened,
there is nothing that escapes from sight.

*Glaukos*: glowing, brightly gleaming
*Glaux*: fierce glittering like the eyes of a field owl
    that fit in perfectly with willow, olive, grape.

It more sparkles than shines,
is more twinkle than glow;
I don't know what the field owl thinks of it.

Nearly touchable, the sun burns its light
into high, narrow windows of the cathedral,
Unearthly the source and yet at this place
transformed by glass and space
into the reflection of a world
that no longer exists.

The master builder created it,
the writer described it –
with flutes and drums it was revered.
    The delicate sound of polyphonic song
rehearsed in parts in the cold dawn
by six boys and some monks.
    The Romanesque choir – subdued
by Gothic slenderness, glass, flying buttresses,
all that delight in building can achieve with space –
offered a hymn to light
through the grey-coloured day and rose
above the rough lives of tramps and peasants on the outside.

While pure throats sang their hearts out, a freezing
congregation sometimes dozed for hours, feasting
on dreams of ham and wine in great abundance.

In spite of pride and lechery, the masters
of polyphony did create, earthly and clear,
a heavenly song of light.

2

Aquinas, Duns Scotus, Robert Grosseteste –
they polished a language of refined thoughts,
described the layering and magic of the light,
its fracturing and colour, form and number,
*claritas* en *visio*, clarity and understanding
  of the mysterious gleam
   from a godlike universe.
Super-terrestrial glow, but also an inner flame
that rises from the core of things
and the warmth of a human heart.

4

The poet, wise or weird, is imitator and composer
  (says Gregory of Nazianzus).
Poetry is a myth in music, she suffers
from a deficiency of truth
  (the brain Aquinas states).
Metaphors produce lies ...
Perhaps there is an eye for coloration
and luminous bodies that spread human splendor          splendor formae humanitas
  (writes Albertus Magnus, standing at his lectern).
Through light and lust, sparks will leap over,
fires will flame up that without love would not ignite.

5

Robert Grosseteste, bishop of Lincoln, turned himself
from underprivileged lad into a powerful philosopher, studied
in Oxford and Paris, spoke three languages, wrote 'De Luce' –
about the laws of light and the dimensions of space:
that light as the primary substance controls the universe,
multiplies and spreads throughout the cosmos.

As at night the northern sky flamed up before his eyes,
veils of light blew along the horizon,
the divine sun on a summer day became
a fire-spitting body, fed by an unknowable force,
by an eternal source that invisibly, behind the sun,
provided the firmament with stars and comets.

Robert kept monks and monasteries under his thumb,
he was a strict man, feared for severe visitations.
His life knew no ecstasy, as a prelate he was
hated, as a scholar revered. Few read
his words, his books did not spread
like the light he had so minutely described.

Desire for wisdom and insight
did not reconcile him in the least
with God's other servants.
He let the Curia have it, denounced
the brutal avarice of cardinals
and had some strong words for the Pope.

Robert Greathead died in 1255, he came out of the 12ᵗʰ century,
lived to be very old, retaining a sharp mind.
His cosmogony was highly thought of
and assured of future fame.
Other than a Prince of the Church, outsiders saw
above all a formidable thinker.

6

*Lux* is the foundation. Is light that radiates strength.
*Lumen* is called the light that spreads through air and space
*Splendor* is the brilliance of transparent things
or a body that is made diaphanous.
*Supersplendere* ... a sparkling that surpasses everything,
a heavenly vision.

I am the nominalist
who names and covers everything in words.
I say the names and appropriate the things.
The words & things: yeast for the mind,
a singing for the sake of singing, splendor –
feast of light, a glow through the stained windows.

Did Foucault not come centuries too late?
Ockham is my master, Abélard my mate.

10
SPLENDOR

Leaves fallen on a dune trail, dwarf oaks,
then pines: walking bouncily
on a bed of needles. A distant path
silvers between drinking hole and sand-drift.
Fire smoulders in the eye,
the evening sun lighter, slowly sinking
and white-shining behind trees –
so different from the greyish morning.

Lost in light, the unearthly material,
I find myself again in growing darkness.
A foot glides stiffly over tepid sand,
  a blue-ish glow lights up beneath my shoes
at the high-water mark.
  The white of igniting carbide in a boat,
the reflection in water, the splendour of fires
fed by some nighttime bathers.

Seaweed lies like stargrass on the beach,

I practise the song of the earth, despise
this world not yet.

*Verklärte Nacht …*

The shining sea and the slow swell
of taking and giving in abundance or need.

There is a life that shrinks and diminishes.
There is a light that neither fades nor vanishes.

# Field Notes from Underground

## Speaking in Tongues

I have never consciously used the subterranean as a motif or theme. Although everything that arose in the mind was based on everyday life, it was the reality of the imagination that was speaking, the intuition of the moment that guided the writing hand. But an initiate of the literary underground enlightened me: he reminded me that more would have gone on in the caverns of the mind than I realized at the time.

The situation in which we now find ourselves differs greatly from the one in the already distant but still so recent past. The bondage of the citizen, the first signs of which were noted more than sixty years ago by Gabriel Marcel in *Man Against Mass Society*, can be called complete. And with that the subjugation to anonymous forces and powers controlling everything. At the same time the pressure of the world has increased, while the world itself has become unrecognizable to many: chaotic, lacking in solidarity, riddled with self-interest, digital pleasure and violence. And yet it is still the same world. Intelligence and stupidity have always battled for priority, with the last one all too often the winner. Under our feet is still the same combustible volcano, growling and rumbling in the depths and we are once again the dancers on the fragile crust that covers the crater. Am I arguing for a new *danse macabre*? You would nearly think so. But there is also the dance of the word, expressed by the ageing but oh so vigorous shaman who is singing his lungs out and imagines that he is (sometimes) subduing the bad, untameable forces of the underworld...

> A speaking in tongues as if the ecstasy
> still persists,
> euphoria is not suppressed
> and the soul not out of touch with fire –

as if the water is not up to our lips,
the language unsullied, the image
uncorrupted, the spirit
untamed and the pure song
   sung again.

A speaking in tongues, while the world
crushes life and, dancing gleefully,
no longer restrained by anything,
indulges in the lust of killing –

From: Veldnotities uit het souterrain I / Field Notes from Underground I (a fragment)

## Of the Fire God & the Mortal (I)

Who lives in the navel of the earth,
  in the heart of the volcano?
It is the very old god:
    his intestines are upset,
he is vomiting from all his crater mouths.
  Ay, let's pour pulque for him,
pulque, mezcal and fresh blood,
so that his cramps let off, his flatulence subsides
and he will dreamlessly, deeply intoxicated
  sleep for years.
His fiery heart is no longer playing up,
the cone cap radiates peace & quiet,
sleep smooths out all his wrinkles.
  Ayah!

The very old god lives in the navel of the earth,
  in the heart of the volcano.
He who no one knows, who created gods in darkness
warms himself by the glow, the fire
that deep under the mountains in hidden hearths is raging,
  fire that rarely dies
but sparks and spews
when I, a mortal, stop singing,
disdain the flower, despoil the earth.
  The heart is tranquilized,
the knife is being sharpened,
the butterfly descends on the flower.
The song flourishes, its sweet smell
  will intoxicate us. Ayah!

From: Veldnotities uit het souterrain II / Field Notes from Underground II

141

## Of the Fire God & the Mortal (II)

The very old god is shaking with anger,
out of spite he crawls deep into the crater
towards a whirling lava sea.

The angry god disappears in smoke and fire,
he rebukes the people, he rebukes the world,
rakes like a stoker in the hearth of the volcano.

Singing between fumaroles I descend:
my song will appease him,
through my song he will calm down.

His hot breath singes my skin,
a lava tongue licks at my shins,
malignant steam escapes from hardened soil.

Pulque and peyote temper fear,
alleviate pain. Far from myself I'm on
the road to where nothing will be left.

The fire churns in the depths, flames
dance and suffocate – crimson-red
plumes rise up from bleeding rock.

The god is blazing mad, he throws up bile
and ash over the earth that blackens.
I offer my word, I offer myself

to quench his scorching heart.
Ay, my song flames up, his breath
turns sulphurous, my life dies out
    in order to save fields and cities:
    there is no reconciliation
    unless in death.

* * *

What am I getting myself into? These songs about the Lord of the Fire contrast in many ways with what has also fascinated me in the European culture of the Middle Ages. The obsession with death, as expressed through the so-called dance of death ('danse macabre'), the 'memento mori' ('remember that you must die') and the imagined journey underground where the dead are joyfully greeted by the moles. But this obsession with death was just as characteristic of the Aztec culture of the same period, even though it was experienced and expressed in a totally different way. So it's no wonder that in a dusty corner of my mind slumbered the memory of an old figure from the Mexican underworld. In the form of spectacular terracotta figurines he can be seen in several museum collections. If he is still alive, he lives underground 'in the navel of the earth', probably in a Smoking Mountain (Popoca-tépetl) from where he wields his influence and authority over the people. His name is Huehueteotl (pronounced: Way-way-tay'-otl). He is the fire god who is also identified as Xiuhtecuhtli (Shee-oo-te-coo'-tli) – a figure who in appearance and vigour differs greatly from him and is sometimes represented with an old head on a young body. This is not exceptional. Many Mexican gods present themselves under different names and with different appearances. Although no religion is simple or unambiguous, it applies in particular to the old, highly developed Mesoamerican cultures, where there was the willingness to integrate the gods of a subjugated neighbouring people into one's own religion. The influence of the old Toltecs on the Aztecs abundantly testifies to that. This merging goes far back in time and explains the presence of a confusing number of gods, who quite often share tasks and functions with each other. They are not supernatural but superpersonal and represent all aspects of life and nature.

Although he resides underground, Huehueteotl, in the Aztec pantheon, is in the first place the keeper of the fire. After a cycle of fifty-two years all fires had to be extinguished. Twelve days of fasting, fear and darkness followed. Would time, and with that life, come to an end? As soon as the bright star Aldebaran passed the zenith on the twelfth night, the world was saved and festivities could erupt. During a ritual in the city of Tenochtitlán, priests would light the new fire on the breast of a captured warrior, whose

143

heart and blood had been sacrificed to the old god. From there the fire was spread across the whole realm. Life was assured for another fifty-two years.

The most important characteristic of Huehueteotl – who is already present around twelve hundred years before the Aztecs – is symbolized on terra cotta figurines by the brazier or fire pan he wears on his head. His face is furrowed, his brow wrinkled. He has a hawk's nose and a pointed beard, his tongue is sticking out of a toothless mouth. Round earplugs improve his repellent appearance somewhat.

The startling thing is that we are dealing here with an archaic, androgyne god, who is called 'in Totan, in Tota', meaning: 'our mother – our father'. Although he resides 'in the shadows of death', he differs fundamentally from the god who controls the underworld (Mictlan) and makes the dead disappear. So Huehueteotl is both man and woman, which would indicate that the god(dess) as a duality has been active in a creative form from the beginning of mankind. It is said of this divine creature that it first 'invented itself', before it brought about the other gods and creatures – the omnipresent, twofold Ometeotl being one of them.

The principle of duality would largely determine the organization of the everyday Aztec world. The god himself however was 'invisible like the night, intangible like the wind'. Duality and truth were according to the brilliant Mexico-scholar Miguel Léon-Portilla his essential characteristics. Everything else was 'like a dream'. As a melancholic Aztec poet once sang, life was as uncertain as it was unreal.

*We come here to sleep,*
*We are awakened to dream,*
*Our body is a flower.*

In other words: we grow up to wither and to come to terms with death. But we also awaken in death from a dreamt existence.

A sacred song or a hymn to the fire god was not known to me. That's why I had no other choice but to write a couple of hymns myself. The notion of the song as a flower with its accompanying symbols was derived from the poetic traditions of the Aztecs.

144

# Lost in Mictlan

Where the dogs lead our souls
in the cold twilight of the North
on the plain of dead grass, there,
   in the beyond, we'll sink away under the ground.

Ay, I roam around now, fearful,
de-fleshed, in phantom light
the dog goes ahead of me – a strong wind
   bites cold like lava glass in my face.

Our fate is set when we come into the world.
We descend and have to wander for four years
among owls and spiders and broken creatures in the night.
   I sing a lamentation on the Shore of the Nine Streams.

The darkness deepens, I wade through
the Nine Waters to where the god
Mictlantecuhtli and his wife already wait for me
   at the gate of disappearance.

Ay, his eyes are bulging, night glasses
through which he sees the drifters sharply.
Before the gate of disappearance
   a last, dim glow of light is now extinguished.

The couple of Mictlan conjure swarms
of ashen souls away without a trace.
Will we ever come back?
   My song makes me, the singer, shiver.

\* \* \*

Fear of the underworld held the Aztecs in its grip. This isn't any less true of
the contemporary Mexican, with the difference that a whole other
underworld has now become a violent upperworld that in recent years has

145

demanded more human sacrifices than the Aztec gods ever did in the course of two centuries.

This song is about Mictlan, the Region of Mystery and the realm of the dead, which obsessed the people of ancient Mexico. It contradicts the often voiced notion that the Mexican Indians were rather indifferent towards death. Nezahualcóyotl (Fasting Wolf) – the famous poet and ruler of Tezcoco – repeatedly expressed himself about the fleetingness of earthly existence and his deep-seated fear of what awaited him in Mictlan. 'My heart is sad,' he writes. 'Ah, it is overcome by sadness. / I am singer on the Shore of the Nine Streams.' In a farewell song this royal poet laments that 'there, on the other shore' he has to descend to the subterranean realm of death. He realizes 'with contracting heart' that he will 'depart and disappear'.

The body was burned or buried, the soul departed to a region that knew many names, but to everyone meant the irreversible 'beyond'. Nine rivers had to be waded through to pass the gate to oblivion in the ninth district of the underworld. The journey there took four years and could not be done without accompaniment, which is not unusual in the mythologies we know. The underworld is mostly reached with the help of a guide. With the Aztecs this task is performed by a mythic dog. At the end of the journey the Lord and Lady of the realm of the dead awaited the souls of the departed. Mictlantecuhtli (Mees-tlan-tay-coot'-li) and Mictecacihuatl (Mees-tay-ca-see'-watl) are their names. The last one was also the mistress of owls and spiders.

Already early, in Pre-Aztec times, the Lord of Mictlan was pictured as an earthenware skeleton. Sometimes with an egg-shaped hat and crossed arms that were resting on bony knees, at other times with a firestone knife in his hand and a vase or censer on his back. The skeleton's head had nearly always two round marble-like eyes, with which he could see the wandering souls in total darkness.

Not everyone was banished to the underworld. Two groups were exempted: on one side the warriors, on the other the farmers, together with people who had met an accidental death and women who had died during childbirth. The warriors were 'eagle companions' who served the sun cult and the war god Huitzilopochtli. Four years after their death they were reborn as honey birds and would fly eternally from flower to flower.

The farmers worshipped the rain god Tlaloc ('Wine of the earth') on whom they depended completely. After death they went to Tlalocan, the paradise 'in the damp warm gardens of the east'. Those who had been struck by lightning or had not survived childbirth were chosen to share this blissful happiness with them. It is not known if members of the religious and cultural-political elite of the Aztec empire managed to avoid the death journey through Mictlan. However beautiful and personal, the songs of king Nezahualcóyotl rely for a large part on the art of rhetoric and stylized lamentation. It seems unlikely that together with the masses of 'common' souls, he would have been condemned to the Region of Mystery.

# The Four Hundred Hares

Fed up and sick from drink and women,
utterly defeated by top Aztecs
   from the city of Tenochtitlán
the prince-rebel of Tlatelolco threw himself
   inebriated from the great temple
taking his favourite dwarf and talisman with him in death.

August 17, 1473

Drugs and drink were denied to the Nahua,
there was stern discipline and punishment.
The law was rough and hard, the same as life.
   In spite of that they did enjoy
   the divine mushroom
   and the mescal in peyote.

Only at sacrifices, ritual fanfare and amusement
was one allowed to smoke and drink, get intoxicated.
But the under-age pulque drinker would be held
   over a burning pepper bush.
   The smoke singed his lungs,
   which quickly made him repent.

Caught again with alcohol
death by stoning would await him.
   Whoever made it to seventy
was allowed to get drunk with impunity.
Providing it was done discretely, free sex
and adultery by wild seventy-year-olds were allowed too.

Ten to twenty hares were cause for merriment,
a hundred hares made old drinkers
forget the sadness and cruelty of life
for a few hours.

Antonio de Mendoza had it drawn and described
   for posterity.
The daughter takes a drunken mother by the arm,
the son supports an intoxicated father on his mat.
She is muttering nonsense on her knees beside the jug,
foolish words crawl fat like worms from his mouth.

Each day he puts a cup of wine
to his parched lips.
He desires and sleeps with the country woman
from the house of corn,
his wife seduces a proud hunter
who passes by with bow and feather headdress.

   She still knows what to do:
   paces up and down with painted face, pretending to be shy.
   A timid greeting, some enticing gestures with her hand,
   a beckoning with her eyes, she lifts
   her eyebrows into crescents
   as if to ask him something.
   She shows her laugh, her butterfly mouth.
   throwing all her charms into the battle.
   When the desire becomes too much for him
   she gives away her body.
      There she lies, stretched out,
   she now undoes her wrap skirt
   and bares her breasts.
   A jade bird on a feather mat.
   A woman so sweet you could eat her,
   a precious flower of roasted corn.
   She has the scent of steaming cacao
   that comforts sad lovers, bringing them joy.

At which the man with heavy
tongue confesses: I was a red
songbird with a supple throat.
Now I drink and sing,
drink and sing myself into oblivion –
I sink into delirium
that delivers me
and makes me disappear.
In bondage to the City Lords
life was like a burden
    of temple stones on my back.
I see four hundred jumping hares,
here and in the grass over there.
My sons are watching
and no longer holding me.
Do they drink maguey sap with me
that the goddess prepared?
    She has four hundred sons
    who are the shadow beings of the hares.

I let myself go and laugh
    about all that
    the capriciousness of a cruel existence
    has never brought.

Is this a trap?
Do I deceive myself perhaps?
Has a strange power robbed me
    of my senses?
A jug rolls empty on the ground.
The straw-covered-mirror shows a dream
    of love and combat in the night.
My head is spinning, flashing.

I am petrified with fear
   as if the sovereign god who mocks us
   has drafted me once more
   and spat me out like a drunken warrior on a battlefield.

* * *

It is cooler here then above ground. Still, it will sometimes get to me. Drink
and the outside heat will go to my head. Is my age finally making itself felt
through dizziness? 'You will grope around in the afternoon heat', a poet
from the recent past predicted. It's an observation I can only endorse. In
spite of that, I don't yet see hares, or rabbits for that matter. One chronicler
from the past speaks of hares, an other one sticks to rabbits. In both cases
they measure the state of drunkenness in which those earlier Mexicans
could find themselves. Four hundred hares, or perhaps rabbits, meant
oblivion, total intoxication.

   The alcoholic beverage called pulque was responsible for the heightened
state of merriment that a melancholic Aztec could experience. Pulque –
ochtli in Nahuatl – is fermented agave sap, erroneously mistaken for 'wine'
by Spanish chroniclers. There were several pulque gods. The 'With-straw-
covered-mirror' (Tezcatzontécatl) is mentioned in the poem, as is the
goddess of the maguey or agave plant (Mayahuel).

   Antonio de Mendoza, viceroy of New Spain, commissioned a codex that
was completed in 1542. It's a beautiful pictographic document in which all
kinds of scenes relating to Aztec rituals and behaviours are truthfully
shown. Among it the carefree imbibing of pulque by men and women
above seventy.

The first stanza refers, in a condensed way, to a complicated affair, in which
drink, women and violence played a role. In 1473, the wayward and
perverted Lord of Tlatelolco (the prosperous trade centre of the country)
hatched a plot against the central power of the Aztec empire. He staged a
coup that spectacularly failed. It turned out that the highest authorities of
the neighbouring city Tenochtitlán through betrayal and close family ties
were completely in the know of the planned military action. The boasting

by the plotter had not gone unnoticed either.

The successful strategist and builder of the empire, Tlacayélel (Clear Nature) was in spite of his advanced age greatly superior to his opponent. The same went for the commander of Tenochtitlán Axayacatl (Water Face). Their opponent Moquihuixtl (Trembling Eye) enjoyed a dubious reputation as the lascivious leader of Tlatelolco who neglected and humiliated his aristocratic wife publicly and made her sleep on the ground in rags. In the meantime he amused himself daily with drink and numerous women who had to oblige him at any time. After an envoy from Tenochtitlán had been brutally beheaded by the right hand of Trembling Eye a confrontation was unavoidable.

During the short, but fierce nighttime collision, Trembling Eye threw a group of naked young women into the battle. They walked up to the enemy and had to push up their breasts with their hands to confuse and seduce the warriors. Pursued by the elite forces of Water Face, the rebel of Tlatelolco fled to the high temple plateau. According to apocryphal sources, he committed suicide there, 'sick from too much alcohol'. A more official historical account states that the victors threw the decadent plotter off the temple. In order to complete the humiliation, the temple pyramid became a public toilet (!), the city lost its autonomy while the innocent population had a heavy tribute imposed on them.

The cocoa or chocolatl was an exquisite drink that, especially in higher circles, was drunk at special occasions, but was also enjoyed as a delicacy in solid form. Like a few other luxury and food items, chocolate was unknown in Europe until the Spanish conquest of Mexico.

About the erotically charged songs of the Aztecs, it finally has to be noted that there is sometimes mention of a 'alegradora' or 'ahuiani': a woman of pleasure. In the passage with the enticing older woman who seduces a 'proud hunter' some lines are quoted from an erotic poem that was created in the second half of the fourteenth century. It has been recorded as 'Tlaltecatzin's Song' and conjures up the memory of unforgettable meetings with a young prostitute. The aging singer/poet thinks back with melancholy to this 'sweet and delightful woman', whom he got to know in Tezcoco. He himself held a high office in the surroundings of this city. Peaceful Tezcoco, an important political-cultural centre, was deeply influenced by the old Toltec culture and the world of ideas of king Quetzalcóatl (not the god of that name) who had been driven out. Typical for the poet and ancient Mexican poetry in general is the connection between erotic rapture and thoughts about death. In 'Tlaltecatzin's Song' the warm memory of the once so young woman is immediately followed by a feeling of mortality. The body decays and is doomed to die. Eros and Thanatos come together in the song.

# Tramontane

Imbued with the physical necessity
        to give shape to an inner landscape
    in the face of destruction and demolition,
      knowing
        that we can't live
    without demolition and decomposition
you work on in seclusion
        to unlock the landscape
      up to the limit of the visible
          where you advance step by step
                like a tactile being
      with antennas
and sometimes retrace your steps
       to erase
      the tracks and imprints that you left behind.

2

Like a shaman awaking on a mountain top
        from a sleep full of terror
    you come to your senses;
                a *zerstückelter mensch*                    *crumbled being*
who belies his fragmentation
    in the poem
            that dispossesses the maker, enlightens
and cures him of a world
        that undermines the foundation of all its
            subtly variegated manifestations
        and unbalances the earthbound man,
            making thinking suspect,
        subjugating the body to alien constraint –
in its demeanor there is nothing peaceful,
                it even strives for peace with violence.

From: *Nieuwe gedichten / New Poems*

# Nine Good Reasons Why I Cannot Write an Introduction*

## Breyten Breytenbach

1

Dear Hans ten Berge,
   You are admirably served by the knowledge, the sensitive, seasoned ear
and tongue of Pleuke Boyce. Her 'translations' are sublimed in poetry. Your
verses and other texts, so powerful in the original and so much part of who
and what and where you are – a trajectory of exploration, restless at times
but always sharing a feast of discovery – come to the reader in this
authentic garb as if born and raised in English. One reads them as if they
were naked in their original skin! I will take a risk and say they probably
make the female dimension of the male poet, you here, palpable. It takes
two to dance. And in Pleuke Boyce you have found someone both initiating
and following the steps so that it is difficult to know who leads whom. Does
it matter?
   Any third person wishing to 'introduce' the to-and-fro, the courting and
the dances of a dynamic relationship must be an imposter promoting a
proxy experience, a hair on the soup, a barker trying to entice people to a
show they cannot possibly miss, a 'tongue' too many selling sardines in
Sardinia…
   This would be my first consideration for not being qualified to take a
reader into these texts that are so self-explanatory and pure.

2

I don't recall now where I first met you. It must have been before I was
caught in Nomansland and handed my nine-years prison sentence, because
I remember you as among those who stood shouting on the shore, who
urged me not to be foolish, to come back 'home'. After that there are salient
moments (too few): our paths crossing in the elsewhere which is always the
here. When you came to South Africa to participate in a movable feast of

* This is the shortened version of a more extensive essay.

157

poetry, bringing wisdom and insights that could not be translated, not yet, a fellow-poet presented you as, "le Néerlandais Hans ten Berge, poète mystique de grande érudition." How could I be so presumptuous as to want to 'introduce' a mystic and a scholar? I can only point at the moon and trust I'm not adding half an inch of non-essential flesh to the finger distracting Reader and obscuring the view.

Because it all starts and ends with a clear view stretching to and encompassing – and 'creating' - infinity.


3

And yet we are still here. We have been here for a very long time. Have we gained any traction? Can we say we have come anywhere near the fulfilment of the dreams we had when we were young? Are we even the same people? Was there ever anything to achieve? We look at the portraits of the predecessors, mostly because we *recognize* something there – a similar whistling in the dark, a sidelong glance at a dim mirror, the taste of the bitter tongue in the mouth, the mountain lurking at the front door (even in Holland!) and the marshes at the back. And then we gird our loins as it were : the 'job' of creating or accompanying sequences of consciousness, of recognizing and forging images, of bringing to light the sense if not the purpose of being with the knowledge that there can be no *sense* except the resistance to whatever the alternative may be – this we cannot shake off.

You have continued because there are sounds calling us from the mountain, and light is giving it shape? And then you 'remember' the history of caves and hunters and explorers and kingdoms and myths and maybe even struggles for clarity and the acceptance of compassion. And the paucity and the richness of our words. There is no need for me to *justify* your curiosity, the incompleteness of understanding, the obdurate desire to survive and discover, the *texture* of living and the *rhythms* of disappearing? Yet I do, since you leave traces, and then you see these are also very much those of the nomads and the fugitives who precede you.


4

To my mind comes a snippet of words left behind by the enigmatic poet, Paul Valet, homeless and stateless but a great combatant in the cause for liberty:

158

*When you are your own*
*living target,*
*it is difficult to take aim*
*and not miss.*

How more likely, then, for the critic, or introducer, to misjudge aim, target and the mysterious beauty of the process?

5

Poetry is not self-expression, or absorption in the toys and distractions of the so-called global village—advertisement, apps, mass tourism, facebook, start-ups, identity politics, television, political debates, space travel. Yours, on the contrary, is a matter of consciousness-making, *naked seeing*. And we are awakened, reminded of this as images and illusions mutate line by line. This is what you do in the volume I have in my hands. The truth is, if Truth be told, that you are fighting the 'demons', casting them out, binding and delivering them, putting them to the test of the tongue, putting the curse and the cure of poetry on them. It's beautiful, it's scary.

6

Let me try again: I'm advancing the hypothesis that your poems are vectors of life. It is so that here they may report the immobile travels of the scholar monk. Or, more likely, the pirate. The world traveller who ended up deep in the country and is now reconstituting his journeys and his voyages and his flights. His treasures. But these are not remembrances or meditations – they are being-scapes taking shape and sound and shadow as they appear on the paper. For the first time? Was the treasure chest not always there, waiting to be opened? *Quién sabe?* The reader, who may be a robber at heart, watches through the window of the world unfolding in the movements of the poet. And the reader does not know if he or she is looking *in* or *out*. As you write: "This is it. This is where I lay my life down. This is where it becomes public private public property. This is where the 'frozen' ecstasy and the horror *as from dead lovers, surprised in the act of coition and not found again by friends*, the longing and the joining, are one in time unwriting timelessness, *still expecting birth and already into death*."

You travel to discover what you know. And write to uncover what *is*. Is it endless? Or do you hold the beginning and the end of endlessness in your hands? Put like this we do not need time to have lived. You are making infinity grow. Your poems *are*. They escape interpretation.

7

We need to breathe. Our existence is an inner journey toward nakedness covered with the patchwork of an endless 'outside'. This will continue (we can't go on; we must go on) and as we give direction to our meandering by leaving cairns of stones, by cleaning the mountain, sometimes by burnishing our weapons, by situating the horizons, by singing the praises of the shaman perched in the tree to intervene with fate on our behalf... we glance at one another in passing, we tip a hat, we notice the tearstains on our sleeves, we enquire after our health and that of our faithful translators whom we try to emulate, we wonder (sometimes aloud) whether *cofid* is here to stay – but we know the answer since we live towards death and we hope to imbue both with the transport of beauty. And then we go on for as long as we can or may. Making a noise to let the snakes know about our passing. To chase away the politicians.

8

Your poem, as vessel for texture and rhythm and open-ended movement, posits the fine art of having neither purpose nor the promise of paradise. And yet it fills a very existential need the way a boatload of refugees fills the sea. The sum total of a poem is not suspended belief; it is rather the up-ended belief going to ruin on the white pages folded away in the archives of memory or the reports of border police. It will be the shipwreck you may say, bearing with my hyperbole, once the lines suspending it over the topography of meaning (and of flight) have been snapped from the god-wanting hand of 'before' and 'after'.

9

All this is what I want to talk about but can't. And why would you want me to sit down and take your precious poetry on my lap to be introduced?
Even so, I wish to return to the reluctance I mentioned in my first point

– and to which I then clung as a slippery rope out of the labyrinth of metaphors, the sea perhaps: these poems speak of a great soul's anguish about the human history and trajectory, about *la condition humaine*. They (the texts) do so with dignity and wisdom and, one may say, not with resignation but with a given acceptance. Certainly also as a celebration of the human capacity to express and to encapsulate in our most ancient manifestation of litany and praise-songs and attempts to exorcise that which we cannot know (and even more poignantly that which we *do know*), namely in (and by means of) *poetry*, so as to fellow-travel with awareness and thereby to creatively shape our fate. Your poems, Ten Berge, *transport* us, your readers and other fellow refugees. Even if, having bought a ticket for Alkmaar we end up among the ruins of Aztec times!

You practise this arcane seeing because the shaman is the exorcist of the tribe. Ultimately, the anciently genetic and timeless need to leave a trace embodies a mournfulness, a keening about what we are, but as well a resurgent regret at leaving the known and the experienced and the remembered. The titular ancestor, Ezra Pound, comes to mind, locked in his silence. And then, immediately, the emblematic figure of Bashō also rises to shake a sleeve and point.

Your poetry is the connecting tissue. What remains in the end is breathing. Your poetry, and the poetry of those who are now dust or ashes or memory or myth or invented knowledge, and whose verses have long since been picked clean by fishes or birds or the politically correct and existentially obtuse – is alive and contemporary because it *breathes*.

Why then would I belabour the obvious? Why 'transcribe' and annotate these ship's journals telling us about the strangeness of having lived? About predicting the past? And practicing— as in poetry —the ascetism where 'inside' and 'outside' are seamlessly one? Except to wish these poems well as they enter the port of our collective memory and our shared projections. May they be safe here. At least for now.

(One puts a little paper schooner to water, carrying a feather, a pebble and a flower. And a strip of paper with a mantra on it. The mantra says: There will be A *speaking in tongues as if the ecstasy still persists, and the soul is not out of touch with fire... of the black gondola burning the water around it.* It is not really of any importance if the text should fade. What was once written will remain. Because it is at once unique – *eenmalig* – and as ancient and true as to be non-original.)

*... to be singing on the Shore of the Nine Streams, the nine rivers we have to wade through in the eternal dark...*

Thank you, Hans ten Berge (and Pleuke Boyce), for the coherence of your verses bringing worlds together, a multitude of pasts continuously presencing, as you move with such effortlessness from myth to the making of new vessels.

And in such a way that the One becomes the Other!

*Breyten Bian Tong, Can Ocells – Paris: 9-9-2020*

# Translator's Acknowledgements

My thanks, first and foremost, to Gary Geddes, the initiator of this project, who tirelessly got everything started and put into place and without whom this collection would not exist. He has been a continuous reader of the translations and has offered many helpful suggestions. On top of that, he has been great in spotting spelling and other errors.

To Richard Olafson, for taking it upon him to publish these Selected Poems.

And last but not least to H.C. ten Berge, who accompanied me the whole way during the translation process and whose elucidations and suggestions were an essential part and greatly contributed to the present form of these translations.

# About the Author

H.C. ten Berge was born in 1938 in Alkmaar, the Netherlands. One of Holland's most important poets, he is the author of a large body of work that includes not only poetry but also novels, novellas, essays and translations. Apart from translating from modern languages, he collected and translated poetry and myths of the Aztecs, Inuit, Eastern Siberian Peoples and First Nations of the Pacific Northwest. He has received many awards for his work, including the most important and prestigious oeuvre prize in the Netherlands, the P.C. Hooft Award.

## About the Translator

Pleuke Boyce was born and grew up in the Netherlands and now lives on Vancouver Island. She received the James S. Holmes Award from the Translation Center at Columbia University for her translations of work by Dutch poet Gerrit Achterberg: *But this Land has no End - Selected Poems*. Her translations into Dutch include seven books by Alice Munro.

# About Breyten Breytenbach

Breyten Breytenbach, born 1939 in Bonnievale, South-Africa, is a poet, prose-writer and painter. He became a French citizen in 1982 after spending seven years in a South-African prison as an anti-apartheid activist. His multifaceted work has been translated into many languages. In 2017 he was the Laureate of the Zbigniew Herbert International Literary Award.

His nomadic life stretches from France and Catalonia to South-Africa and Senegal, where he founded the Goree Institute for African artists and writers. Breytenbach 'clearly is the greatest African poet of his generation' (*The New Yorker*).